THE COLLECTED WORKS OF

JIM MORRISON

POETRY, JOURNALS, TRANSCRIPTS, AND LYRICS

FOREWORD BY
TOM ROBBINS

EDITED AND WITH AN INTRODUCTION BY
FRANK LISCIANDRO

PROLOGUE BY
ANNE MORRISON CHEWNING

HARPER
DESIGN
An Imprint of HarperCollinsPublishers

Plan For Book

Poem & Prose-Poem sections
eq. on Diving
Jamaica
Airports etc.

Excerpts from Journal

Symbolic (ie. No Names) Trial
excerpts

___

Also Appendix of all
song lyrics

New Poems
(American Prayers)

Transcript of Miami Tape

Contents

Foreword
Fireflies of the Apocalypse

Those who know James Douglas (Jim) Morrison only as the electrifying lead singer of The Doors, a sixties rock star with panty-dampening good looks, a penetrating voice, and a stage presence somehow both sultry and spooky, threatening and seductive (a living embodiment of that wounded dark angel who carjacks the midnight dreams of many a postpubescent girl), will likely be surprised to learn that throughout his short life (1943–1971) he considered himself first and foremost a *writer*.

Of course, it's well known that Morrison composed the lyrics of many if not the majority of The Doors' hit songs, lyrics that still prowl the auditory hallways of legions of fans, and are included toward (appropriately) the end (". . . my only friend, the end") of this retrospective. Only recently, however, have surviving family members disclosed that from an early age Jim filled journal after journal (dozens of them!) with copious expressions of an obviously *literary* mind: that he professed, in fact, to have become a musician largely by chance.

Most of the journal entries collected in this exhaustive, engagingly eccentric volume consist of highly poeticized image clusters and versified vignettes: "memories" of a fantasized antiquity, warnings against future defilements, and brief scenes from psychological nature movies that might have scared Smokey the Bear out of his overalls and caused Disney to open an extermination service. (These visions are not to be confused with the several real treatments, also included here, for films that Jim wished either to direct, star in, or both. These last seem influenced by old gunslinger and gangster movies, as do a few of the poems.)

Energizing each and every page is the compulsive creativity of a kind of castaway on a potentially threatening shore, a lost but determined explorer who both courts danger and seeks to exorcize it; who goes out of his way to pluck the strangest fruits, only to polish them with a cotton cloth of innocence.

Simultaneously atavistic and postmodern, these verses are fraught with evocations of our deepest fears, with poisonous vipers and stinging insects, with serial killers and nuclear clouds. Even as we're pulled along expectantly from one lyric-like line to the next (as if passengers on one of Rimbaud's "drunken boats"), we can almost feel the cobra's tongue flick against our bare neck, sense the maniac's eager eyes peering in our kitchen window, listen for the air raid alarm.

Yes, but there's another side to James Douglas Morrison. He flourished in California in the psychedelic sixties, a period like no other, a time when an entire generation seemed to flirt with its neurological destiny—and without benefit of rocket science, sought to orbit the moon. Morrison wrote that "we had a great visitation of energy," proclaimed that the ancient ones' "time has come again," urged readers to "enter again the sweet forest / enter the hot dream." While he deliberately drove down toad-squirmy backroads of primal terror, ecstasy was often naked in the shotgun seat, spinning jeweled pinwheels, peeling a peach.

Poets—the ones who actually matter—have seldom hesitated to play with fire. For Rumi, it was the fire of spiritual longing, for Whitman the celebratory heart-blaze of brotherhood. Rimbaud heated his images over live coals of voluntary madness, Blake could fantasize about an orange tiger "burning bright, in the forests of the night" (though Wordsworth seemed warmed enough by the pale yellow radiance of daffodil fields). The myriad, often disconnected verses of Morrison seem less like a bonfire than shower after shower of cerebral sparks, loosely associated embers "setting the night on fire."

Or maybe not.

Jim's images, while certainly scattered, are more dense than sparks; less inclined to disintegrate or simply drift away. Lit by either a kind of existential dread, a mythological rapture, or both, they resemble more precisely swarms of cerebral fireflies: those existential lightning bugs that flicker on and off, off and on, down in the black velvety night of deepest human consciousness. Lantern lice of our lost Eden. Fireflies of the apocalypse.

Tom Robbins

Introduction
Thoughts in Time

When people discover that I knew and worked with Jim Morrison, they invariably ask me, "What was he really like?"—a seemingly simple question that is always hard to answer.

I knew several Jims: the shy loner who was my classmate at the UCLA School of Film; the rock performer who was always raising the stakes of what was culturally acceptable; the lyricist, poet, and writer who surprised me with notebook pages of complex poems and gifts of self-published books; and the hitchhiker:

> Thoughts in time & out of season
> The hitchhiker stood by the side
> of the road
> & leveled his thumb
> in the calm calculus of reason

This invocation, or incantation, appears as the opening lines of several of Jim's poems. As I read it, he is sketching a portrait of the mid-twentieth-century Dionysus, watching and waiting for the next ride on the infinite highway—his thumb, like a compass, pointing to the next direction; his mind, empty of preconceptions; a man, secure in his calm and measured reason. Jim embellished this image of the hitchhiker in his film treatment "The Hitchhiker: An American Pastoral" and portrayed the character in his film, *HWY*.

In life Jim traveled light and often alone, hitching rides on LA streets, open to whatever chance encounter might satisfy his limitless curiosity and his search for new boundaries.

•

Almost everything Jim wrote was first set down in a notebook or on any handy scrap of paper: a cocktail napkin, an empty page at the back of a book, a creased envelope. The notebooks came in a variety of sizes and shapes: from steno pads and old-fashioned ledgers to school composition books and leather-covered artist's sketch pads. The wealth of material includes poems and songs, short monographs, theater pieces, scenarios, recalled dreams, epigrams, aphorisms—even a diary of his (in)famous trial in Miami.

After Jim's death, many of his notebooks were brought from Paris by Pamela Courson. When she passed away three years later, they were safely stored by her father, Columbus "Corky" Courson. Corky hired me and my then-wife, Kathy, to curate and transcribe works from the notebooks to create a manuscript he hoped to have published. He eventually found a publisher in Villard Books who brought out *Wilderness* (1988) and *The American Night* (1991).

Twenty years later, with the support and participation of Pamela's mother, Pearl Courson, and Jim's sister, Anne Morrison Chewning, I assembled *The Collected Works of Jim Morrison*, a more complete anthology of Jim's writings. Reading and studying the notebooks for a second time gave me an appreciation for the unswerving critical sensibility he brought to the practice of the craft. He often composed multiple drafts of a poem, tightening the line, sharpening the rhythm, and pushing the poem a little closer to sinewy elegance with each draft.

The original plan and sustaining concept for this volume was to release all of Jim's finished writings as well as some that were in progress at the time of his death. At least a third of the material—most of which has never been published—comes directly from the more than thirty notebooks and hundreds of loose handwritten pages that have been archived since Jim's death. This book also includes Jim's three self-published books—*New Creatures*, *The Lords*, and *An American Prayer*—as well as the film treatment for *HWY* and other writings he released during his lifetime.

Everything on Jim's handwritten pages was transcribed exactly as he composed them. As the manuscript's editor, I followed two guidelines: the first was not to change anything, to present the material exactly as it exists. The second, and more difficult to adhere to, was to trust the poet. When I found a poem inscrutable, I trusted that the poet knew what he was creating. Along the way I was forced to abandon my preconceived notions of what a poem should be and understand Jim's poetry for what it was: unconventional, experimental, bold, threatening, often difficult and, for some readers, possibly offensive.

•

When fellow teenagers were struggling with high school essay assignments, Jim was composing poems and making notes about the alchemists and Friedrich Nietzsche. One poem that survived from those years, "Horse Latitudes," shows that Jim was writing accomplished, mature, and crafted verse even then.

In "Horse Latitudes," in a few naturalistic and frightening lines, he depicts what happened in the fifteenth and sixteenth centuries when Spanish galleons transporting horses to their New World colonies lost the wind and idled on becalmed seas. In the poem, the ship's water supply runs low, and the crew is forced to act:

> Awkward instant
> And the first animal is jettisoned,
> Legs furiously pumping
> Their stiff green gallop
> And heads bob up
> Poise
> Delicate
> Pause
> Consent

Jim continued to compile notebooks of poetry and observations throughout his teenage years, but none of those writings have survived. In an interview, Jim revealed that he had disposed of all his early writings. It wasn't until his time at UCLA that he began again to fill notebook pages with poems and short essays.

At the height of his music career, Jim took steps to clear a space in the public view for the poet and writer. He submitted his work to pop and teen magazines and began to organize his writings so that he could self-publish them.

Walking into The Doors' office one day in April 1969, I noticed parcel-paper-wrapped packages stacked three feet high near Jim's desk. He was half sitting on the desktop, a slim book in his hand. Without a word, he handed me the book he was holding, *New Creatures*. Reaching into an open stack, he picked up an inch-thick blue folio, *The Lords/Notes on Vision*, and gave it to me. Both volumes had just been delivered and still carried the bright smell of printer's ink. Jim had not mentioned, nor did anyone know, that he was self-publishing his writings. Prominently embossed on the cover of the thin book and the folio binder was his full name, James Douglas Morrison, marking for the first time the separation he wanted to establish between the writer and the rock performer.

I took the books home and read every page twice, attempting to unwrap the sense and nuance of the poems and the implication of the literary passages. In *The Lords/Notes on Vision*, Jim offers lean expository lines about Cinema & Alchemy, Shamanism & Seances:

> In the seance, the shaman led. A sensuous panic,
> deliberately evoked through drugs, chants, dancing,
> hurls the shaman into trance. Changed voice,
> convulsive movement. He acts like a madman. These
> professional hysterics, chosen precisely for their
> psychotic leaning, were once esteemed.

The antics of a shaman were not tolerated, much less esteemed, by the managers of theaters where rock acts performed in the 1960s. Sometimes when Jim tried to involve his audience and evoke "a sensuous panic" on stage, the person in charge pulled the power plug, darkened the stage, and abruptly terminated the performance. Jim was arrested a couple of times, and in New Haven, Connecticut, the police marched him offstage in handcuffs.

At times, the writing in *New Creatures* resembles news bulletins or reminders of recent history. These lines bring to mind the newsreel murders of the 1960s.

> The assassin's bullet
> Marries the King
> Dissembling miles of air
> To kiss the crown.

In April 1970 when Simon & Schuster combined both of his self-published books in a single volume, *The Lords and The New Creatures*, Jim was delighted. The literary recognition he worked to achieve was finally arriving.

Another self-published book appeared in 1970. *An American Prayer* is a three-by-four-inch chapbook designed to slip easily into the back pocket of jeans. Jim said he formatted the poem that way because he wanted it to be a piece of writing people could travel with. Many of Jim's poems pose questions, and there are so many questions in *An American Prayer* that it often reads like an interrogation. He asks us repeatedly to confirm or at least consider his observations. The poem begins:

> Do you know the warm progress
>   under the stars?
> Do you know we exist?
> Have you forgotten the keys
>   to the Kingdom?
> Have you been borne yet
>   & are you alive?

Near the end of the book Jim explores in metered detail death's sudden and unexpected arrival and the temptation to exchange the slow, often painful decay of the body for a pair of angels' wings.

> Do you know how pale & wanton thrillful
>   comes death on a strange hour
>   unannounced, unplanned for
> like a scaring over-friendly guest you've
>   brought to bed
> Death makes angels of us all
>   & gives us wings
> where we had shoulders
>   smooth as raven's
>   claws

Are these lines a foretelling, a premonition, of his own death? I heard Jim say more than once that life was a trip and he intended to enjoy it for as long as he could.

•

On the night of his twenty-seventh birthday, December 8, 1970, Jim rented a studio at the Village Recorder in West Los Angeles to tape his poetry and a few songs for an album contracted by Elektra Records. He asked music producer and engineer John Haeny to record the session; and he invited a few friends—Kathy Lisciandro, The Doors' secretary; Florentine Pabst, a German journalist; and me—to listen and celebrate with him. I brought a camera.

After almost two hours of reading from typed pages, Jim called a time out: "Okay. Now, let's go get a taco." We walked a couple of blocks to the Lucky U, a Mexican restaurant and bar that was a hangout for UCLA film students. My photos show us taking a break, enjoying tacos and beers, and having a few laughs.

Back in the studio, after another sixty minutes of reading and singing, Jim invited Florentine and Kathy to read with him. They were reluctant until he told them that the poem, "Soldier's Wife's Letter," had a part for women's voices. For a few more minutes they feigned uncertainty, but John Haeny was soon positioning a microphone for them, and Jim was showing them on the typescript pages where he wanted them to start.

The fun began when he asked them to read in unison. A handful of hilarious false starts and the mix of pronunciations—both correct and incorrect—in Florentine's German-accented English and Kathy's Brooklyn accent—had us all in stiches. In time they got the hang of reading together and sailed through a couple of good takes. Jim was enchanted. John, noting the late hour, tried to end the session, but the women insisted on hearing a playback of their reading. They glowed and smiled at each other as they listened to the good takes; then they both insisted on hearing the tracks again.

In the dark early morning, John finally kicked us out so he could shut down the recording console and tape machines. We were tired, yet averse to ending the celebration. Kathy and I drove home to Laurel Canyon quoting—and often misquoting—Jim's visionary phrases and lines to each other.

•

Over the years, I've stopped mentioning the hitchhiker to those who ask me about the "real" Jim Morrison. The concept was too cerebral and abstract and it involved too much explanation. Instead, I suggest that they might find and listen to Jim's interviews and read his poetry.

For a bright and transparently honest view of what it might be like to be Jim Morrison, I recommend taking a trip through "As I Look Back." Quick and compelling, this piece is like an album of snapshots of the struggles, successes, insights, and epiphanies Jim collected along his life's journey.

> Elvis had sex - wise
> mature voice at 19.
>
> Mine still retains the
> nasal whine of a
> repressed adolescent
>   minor squeaks & furies
> An interesting singer
> at best - a scream
> or a sick croon. Nothing
> in-between

Although this book is not about Jim, its pages are filled with closeup and wide-angle views of his world: memory and metaphor woven together, ideas and beliefs knit into lines of poetry, feelings rhymed as song lyrics, observations that evolve as essays and film treatments. Jim captured the occasions and circumstances of his life in his notebooks. We have reproduced those pages in this book exactly as he set his words to paper.

Frank Lisciandro

Prologue

A natural leader, a poet,
A Shaman, w/the
Soul of a clown.
—Jim Morrison, "Road Days"

When I lived in London in 1967, you could hear "Light My Fire" playing everywhere—through apartment doors, from open windows, and in coffee shops. I never realized it was my brother singing until I received a package from my mother. There was no note, just a record album with a large image of my older brother Jim's face front and center on the cover under the title: *The Doors*.

In high school, Jim spent his time writing, reading, doodling, and painting. He liked to listen to comedy records and to play practical jokes. He also liked to make up stories, sometimes incorporating characters or images from fiction he'd read. He once told a group of us kids that the bananafish from J. D. Salinger's famous short story lived in the filter of a neighbor's swimming pool, then led us there to feed them rocks. He bought old blank ledger books and wrote prose poems in them as well as short plays, one of which he read to my mother's astonished bridge group. He shopped in used clothing stores, occasionally skipped school, and hung out at a library or bookstore, where Camus, Genet, and Nietzsche captivated him.

After high school, Jim attended a junior college in Florida, where he lived with our grandparents. He didn't work, living instead on the barest minimum my parents sent him, a transaction that was contingent on Jim sending a monthly letter home. My mother read these letters aloud at dinner, often to our amusement; in a particularly memorable note, Jim wrote that there had been a fire at a local theater and that he had jumped onstage and sang to calm the audience. Of course, we knew that fiction usually trumped truth in these stories.

I had always thought Jim would end up as a penniless beatnik or poet. I'm not sure he ever had a job before The Doors, and I often wondered where he'd be at age fifty. But he ultimately graduated from UCLA, where he studied film. At the time, our family was flung across six thousand miles— from London to Alexandria, Virginia, to LA. In those days, long-distance phone calls were limited to emergencies, so we mostly wrote letters. We didn't hear as much from Jim after he finished at UCLA.

After The Doors' first album came out, I followed Jim's career, loved the music, and, when I returned to California, visited Jim and Pam Courson in LA. Seldom without a notebook and pen, he self-published his poems and published others with Simon & Schuster and in literary magazines. He also recorded them and read them aloud in concert. He wrote a movie script and filmed it with friends. Some of his poetry and his film were personal works, exclusive to him, and some of his writings became an integral part of The Doors' lyrics. He once said to me, "Money is freedom." And that was how he lived; he didn't use the money he earned for material things; he

used it to fund new projects. During their five years together, Jim and The Doors recorded six albums and played live. This was an incredibly creative, productive time.

My brother Andy and I first heard of Jim's death on the radio on July 5, 1971. We didn't want to believe it and thought it was a rumor, like others we'd heard before. Jim had died two days earlier, on July 3 in Paris. Stardom had come so quickly and then, just as quickly, it was over. I never had the chance to see Jim perform—how could I have known things would end so soon?

Jim was buried at Père Lachaise Cemetery, with only Pam and a few friends in attendance. The mystery surrounding his death gave way to a hope that stayed with me for years—perhaps Jim was still alive. But no.

It is difficult for anyone to take over a legacy. After the deaths of both Jim and Pam, my parents and the Coursons were coexecutors of Jim's estate. In 2009 when both of my parents were gone, I became the executor of our half. We decided early on to follow the lead of the remaining members of The Doors when it came to projects related to the band. But when considering what to do with Jim's work, we tried to follow his intent.

Whether to publish his writing posthumously was the first and most important question. As I looked through his journals, I came upon what is now the first page in this volume: "Plan for Book"; it became the blueprint for this collection.

Working with Jim's friend Frank Lisciandro, we gathered Jim's published poems, journal entries, and movie script. We collected lyrics he had written and quotes from various publications and interviews. We also included photos, stills from his unreleased film HWY, and handwritten journal pages. Our goal was never to explain Jim, but to let him tell his story through his own words, images, and interviews.

The making of this book has been a long undertaking and required the help of many people along the way. We can't thank Frank Lisciandro enough for his full dedication to Jim's work and his personal and thoughtful reflections as he edited it. We were honored to have Tom Robbins write the foreword in his singularly intuitive style. My love and thanks to my brother Andy and his wife, Barbara, my husband, Randy, and our kids, Dylan, Tristin, and Sefton, who were always there to organize, read, discuss, and exchange ideas. My thanks to the Courson family, especially Emily Burton and James Burton, as well as Jeff Jampol, Kenny Nemes, and the staff at Jampol Artist Management for supporting us all the way. Finally, I'd like to thank Jennifer Gates, our representative at Aevitas Creative Management, Elizabeth Viscott Sullivan, executive editor at Harper Design, and designers Jonny Sikov and Michael Bierut at Pentagram.

This has been a wonderful collaboration.

Anne Morrison Chewning

I

POEMS
AND
WRITINGS

I think around the fifth or sixth grade
I wrote a poem called "The Pony Express."
That was the first I can remember. It
was one of those ballad-type poems.
I never could get it together, though.
I always wanted to write, but I figured
it'd be no good unless somehow the hand
just took the pen and started moving
without me really having anything to
do with it. Like automatic writing. But
it just never happened.[1]

The Pony Express

The Pony Express carried the mail -
    Over hill, over dale, over rough
    rugged trails.
And the brave men that carried it didn't
complain, for they knew they were helping,
their good countries name.
    They rode and rode through strong
    winds and rain, just to carry the
    mail and build up our name.
Over Indian country and great sandy
plains, they carried the mail and shared
our great fame.

May 21, 1954

"Horse Latitudes" I wrote when I was in high school. I kept a lot of notebooks through high school and college, and then when I left school, for some dumb reason—maybe it was wise—I threw them all away.

There's nothing I can think of that I'd rather have in my possession right now than those two or three lost notebooks. I was thinking of being hypnotized or taking sodium pentothal to try to remember, because I wrote in those books night after night. But, maybe, if I'd never thrown them away, I'd never have written anything original—because they were mainly accumulations of things that I'd read or heard, like quotes from books. I think if I'd never gotten rid of them I'd never have been free.[2]

Horse Latitudes

When the still sea conspires an armor
And her sullen and aborted
Currents breed tiny monsters,
True sailing is dead.

Awkward instant
And the first animal is jettisoned,
Legs furiously pumping
Their stiff green gallop,
And heads bob up
Poise
Delicate
Pause
Consent
In mute nostril agony
Carefully refined
And sealed over[3]

Eyes

He sought exposure, and lived the horror of trying to assemble a myth before a billion dull dry ruthless eyes. Leaving his plane, he strode to the wire fence, against the advice of his agents, to touch hands. Standing close to appeal his invitation for them to admire him w/worship or weapons. The constant unspoken interior knowledge, that his body was target every public second. Charged murderous awareness of beasts. New nerves of sensation flowered on his neck spine garden. When he looked at you, they said, he stripped back your skull. Naturally. For well-wishing admirer smiles easily hide death behind cat teeth. Not paranoia or beyond grave carelessness, but a fine sensuous knowledge of violence in an eternal present.

CYCLOPS. People who resemble primitive lizards have a jewel within their skull. Called the "pineal gland", it is located inside the brain at the juncture of the two hemispheres of cerebellum. In some this third vestigial eye is still sensitive to light.

The eye resists detached analysis. Realize that the eyes actually are two soft globes floating in bone.

The impressions are seeing me.

Ask anyone what sense he would preserve above all others. Most would say sight, forfeiting a million eyes in the body for two in the skull. Blind, we could live and possibly discover wisdom. Without touch, we would turn into hunks of wood.

The eye is a hungry mouth
That feeds on the world.

Architect of image worlds
in competition with the real.

There are twin planets
in the skull.

The eye is god. And the world,
For it has its equator.

Pluck out the animal's eye in the dark and set it down before an object, clear and bright, a window against the sky. The outline of this image is engraved on the retina, visible to the naked eye. This excised eye is a primitive camera, the retina's visual purple acts as emulsion.

Kuhne, following his success with rabbits, was presented the head of a young guillotine victim. The eye was extracted and slit along the equator. The operation was performed in a special red and yellow room. Retina of the left eye offers a sharp but ambiguous image, impossible to define. He spent the next years in search for its meaning, the exact nature of the object, if it was an object.

Windows are eyes of the house. Peer out of your prison body, others peep in. Never a one-way traffic. "Seeing" always implies the possibility of damaged privacy, for as eyes reveal the huge external world, our own infinite internal spaces are opened for others.

What is the fate of the eyes during sleep? They move constantly, like spectators in a theater.

The pupils dilate during abnormal states. Drugs, madness, drunkenness, paralysis, exhaustion, hypnosis, vertigo, high sexual excitement. The eye finding its ocean after the idea of oceans has ended.

Enkidu was a wild man, an animal among animals. One day a woman exposed her nakedness to him at a watering hole, and he responded. That day he left with her to follow the arts of civilization.

Mates are chosen first by visual appeal. Not odor, rhythm, skin. It is an error to believe that the eye can caress a woman. Is a woman constructed out of light or of skin? Her image is never real in the eye, it is engraved on the ends of the fingers.

In the Ars Magna, Great Work, the Alchemist creates the world in his retort.

The eyes are the genitals of perception, and they too have established a tyranny. They have usurped the authority of the other senses. The body becomes a thin awkward stalk to support the eye on its rounds.

Why should the eyes be called "windows of soul" and key to deepest human communion, and touch denied as mild collisions of flesh.

The body is not the house, it is the inside of the house.

The blind copulate, eyes in their skin.

The eye is "light at rest".

(Do we create light in the eye? Is light our own, or from the world?)

In Egyptian mythology the eye is symbol of Osiris, Isis, Horus, and the sun god Ra.

Ptah gave birth to men from his mouth, the gods from his eyes.

City-temple of Brak (3000 B.C.). Discovered thousands of small flat human faces of black and white alabaster, without nose, mouth, ears, but with engraved and carefully painted eyes. Called the Eye Temple: To house these offerings to a divinity.

Oedipus. "Reality" of her naked breasts. Her body.
"You have looked upon those you ought never to
have looked upon." Eyes gouged with a broach from
the dress of dead Jocasta.

Punish the eyes. Shriveled breasts of an old woman. He is led from village to village by a young boy. And everywhere they wait on his words.
Tiresias, said to have spent seven years as a woman, came upon Athene in the forest, bathing. She darkened the intruding eyes.

Saul of Tarsus on the road to Damascus. Blindness elevated him to St. Paul. Why is blindness holy?

Alchemy offers man an original heroism. The Mani taught that man was created as a helper by the messenger of Supreme God of Light to assist by his life and efforts in gathering the scattered, thereby weakened, atoms of light and lead them upward. For light has shone into the darkness and wasted itself and is in grave danger of being swallowed wholly.

Man can assist in the salvation of light.

The process of transforming base metals into gold is called "projection".

In dim light, form is sacrificed for light. In bright light, light is sacrificed for form.

Code of Light. The eye is sick. Pluck it out. The doctor removes the eye to save the body. To do this, he must sever the optic nerve connecting eye with brain. Before anesthesia, it was often reported that the pass of the scalpel created light instead of pain.

Gradually, objects are constructed outside the body.

The eye arises from light, for light. Indifferent organs and surfaces evolve into their unique form. The fish is shaped by water, the bird by air, the worm by earth. The eye is a creature of fire.[4]

The Anatomy of Rock

or
The whole thing started w/
Rock 'n' Roll
Now it's
Out of control

The 1st electric wildness came
over the people
on sweet Friday.
Sweat was in the air.
The channel beamed,
token of power
Incense brewed darkly.
Who could tell then that here
it would end?

One school bus crashed w/a train.
This was the crossroads.
Mercury strained.
I couldn't get out of my seat.
The road was littered
w/dead jitterbugs.
Help,
we'll be late for class.

The secret flurry of rumor
marched over the yard &
pinned us unwittingly
Mt. fever.
A girl stripped naked on the
base of the flagpole.
In the restrooms all was cool
& silent
w/the salt-green of latrines.
Blankets were needed.

Ropes fluttered.
Smiles flattered
& haunted.

Lockers were pried open
& secrets discovered.

Ah sweet music.

Wild sounds in the night.
Angel siren voices.
The baying of great hounds.
Cars screaming thru gears
& shrieks
on the wild road
Where the tires skid & slide
into dangerous curves.

Favorite corners.
Cheerleaders raped in summer
buildings.
Holding hands
& bopping toward Sunday.

Those lean sweet desperate hours.

Time searched the hallways
for a mind.
Hands kept time.
The climate altered like a
visible dance.

Night-time women.
Wondrous sacraments of doubt
Sprang sullen in bursts
of fear & guilt
in the womb's pit hole
below
The belt of the beast.[5]

The Celebration of The Lizard

Lions in The street + roaming
Dogs in heat, rabid, foaming
A beast caged in The heart of a city

The body of his mother
Rotting in The summer ground
He Fled The Town

He went down South
And crossed The border
Left The chaos + disorder
Back There
Over his shoulder

~~Tijuana Rose~~
~~Tijuana Rose~~
~~Nobody knows~~
~~I love you?~~

One morning he awoke in a green
hotel w/ a strange animal groaning
beside him — sweat oozed from its
shiny skin.

The Celebration of the Lizard

Lions in the street and roaming
Dogs in heat, rabid, foaming
A beast caged in the heart of a city
The body of his mother
Rotting in the summer ground.
He fled the town.

He went down South and crossed the border
Left the chaos and disorder
Back there over his shoulder.

One morning he awoke in a green hotel
With a strange creature groaning beside him.
Sweat oozed from its shiny skin.

Is everybody in? *(repeated 3 times)*
The ceremony is about to begin.

Wake up!
You can't remember where it was.
Had this dream stopped?

The snake was pale gold
Glazed & shrunken.
We were afraid to touch it.
The sheets were hot dead prisons.

Now, run to the mirror in the bathroom,
Look!
I can't live thru each slow century of her moving.
I let my cheek slide down
The cool smooth tile
Feel the good cold stinging blood
The smooth hissing snakes of rain. . . .

Once I had a little game
I liked to crawl back into my brain
I think you know the game I mean
I mean the game called 'go insane'

Now you should try this little game
Just close your eyes forget your name
forget the world, forget the people
And we'll erect a different steeple.

This little game is fun to do.
Just close your eyes, no way to lose.
And I'm right there, I'm going too.
Release control, we're breaking through.

Way back deep into the brain
Back where there's never any pain.

And the rain falls gently on the town.
And the labyrinth of streams
Beneath, the quiet unearthly presence of
Nervous hill dwellers in the gentle hills around,
Reptiles abounding
Fossils, caves, cool air heights.

Each house repeats a mold
Windows rolled
Beast car locked in against morning.
All now sleeping
Rugs silent, mirrors vacant,
Dust blind under the beds of lawful couples
Wound in sheets.
And daughters, smug
With semen eyes in their nipples

Wait!

There's been a slaughter here.

                              (siren)

          (Don't stop to speak or look around
          Your gloves & fan are on the ground
          We're getting out of town
          We're going to the run
          And you're the one I want to come)

Not to touch the earth
Not to see the sun
Nothing left to do, but
Run, run, run
Let's run

House upon the hill
Moon is lying still
Shadows of the trees
Witnessing the wild breeze
C'mon baby run w/me
Let's run

Run w/me
Run w/me
Run w/me
Let's run

The mansion is warm, at the top of the hill
Rich are the rooms and the comforts there
Red are the arms of luxuriant chairs
And you won't know a thing till you get inside

Dead president's corpse in the driver's car
The engine runs on glue and tar
C'mon along, we're not going very far
To the East to meet the Czar.

Some outlaws lived by the side of a lake
The minister's daughter's in love with the snake
Who lives in a well by the side of the road

Wake up, girl! We're almost home

Sun, sun, sun
Burn, burn, burn
Soon, soon, soon
Moon, moon, moon,
I will get you
Soon!
Soon!
Soon!

Let the carnival bells ring
Let the serpent sing
Let everything

                                        (bells)

    -fade-

        Desert Night
        Voices of the Fire

We came down
The rivers and highways
We came down from
Forests & falls

We came down from
Carson & Springfield
We came down from
Phoenix enthralled

And I can tell you
The names of the Kingdom
I can tell you
The things that you know
Listening for a fistful of silence
Climbing valleys into the shade

                (tambourines)

"I am the Lizard King
  I can do anything

  I can make the earth stop in its tracks
  I made the blue cars go away

  For seven years I dwelt
  In the loose palace of exile,
  Playing strange games
  With the girls of the island.

  Now I have come again
  To the land of the fair, & the strong, & the wise.

  Brothers & sisters of the pale forest
  O children of Night
  Who among you will run with the hunt?

                    (cries of assent)

  Now Night arrives with her purple legion.
  Retire now to your tents & to your dreams.
  Tomorrow we enter the town of my birth.
  I want to be ready."

Music

-fade-

end[6]

Is everybody in? (3)
The ceremony is about to begin.

_____.

Wake up!
You can't remember where it was.
Had this dream stopped?
The snake was pale gold, glazed, & shrunken.
We were afraid to touch it.
The sheets were hot dead prisons.
And she was beside me, old,
She's, no; young.
Her dark red hair.
The white soft skin.
Now run to the mirror in the bathroom,
Look!
She's coming in here.
I can't live thru each slow century
of her moving.
I let my cheek slide down
The cool smooth Tile.
Feel the good cold stinging blood.
The smooth hissing snakes
of rain!

(Winds)

Man's voice :– Baby, baby.
Woman's voice :– Shhhh. What was that?
Man's voice :– I don't know. Sounds like...

(Laughter)

Once I had, a little game
I liked to crawl, back in my brain
I think you know, the game I mean
I mean the game, called go insane

This little game, is fun to do
Just close your eyes, no way to lose
And I'm right here, I'm going to
Release control, we're breaking thru

Now you should try, this little game
Just close your eyes, forget your name
Forget the world, forget the people
And we'll erect, a different steeple

~~purple~~ caves, cool air heights

pools, foam gardens, servants

~~dogs~~ in the cruel ~~nothing~~ Mourning
                              yards.

(Each house repeats a mold,
     windows rolled, beast car
         locked in against morning.

All now sleeping, rugs silent,
     Mirrors vacant, dust blind
         under the beds

Of lawful couples ~~wrapped~~ wound
     in sheets, & daughters,
         smug w/ semen, eyes
             in their nipples.)

Wait!

There's been a slaughter here.

The mansion is warm at the Top of the hill
Rich are the rooms & the comforts there
Red are the arms of Luxuriant chairs
& You won't Know a Thing Till you get inside.

Some outlaws lived on the edge of a lake
The minister's daughters in love w/ the snake
Who lives in a well by the side of the road
Wake up girl, we're almost home.

We should see the gates by morning
we should be inside by evening

Sun Sun Sun
Burn Burn Burn
Soon Soon Soon

Moon - Moon - Moon
I will get you
Soon
Soon
Soon !

(Tambourines~) ~~⬤⬤~~)

I am the Lizard King

I can do anything

I can make the earth stop
                    in its tracks
I made the blue cars go away.
~~I can make myself invisible or small~~
~~I can reach the farthest star~~
~~I can transform myself at will~~
~~I perform wonders stranger still~~

~~Look!~~
~~This Radiant beach~~
~~& cool jewelled Moon.~~

~~Couples, naked, race along~~ down
~~by its quiet edge.~~

~~And we laugh, like~~
~~Soft mad children~~

~~The Music & Voices~~
~~are all around us.~~

(Pause)

For seven years
I dwelt in the loose
Palace of Exile
(playing strange games w/ the girls of the island)
Now I have come ~~again~~
Again
To the land of the fair
& the strong
& the wise.

Brothers & sisters of the pale forest!
O children of Night!
Who among you will run
With the Hunt?
            — cries of assent —

~~Farewell!~~
~~We're leaving everything behind.~~
~~The city is only a dream now~~
~~all those rooms & disorders.~~

~~The proud sun~~
~~& violent milk-white moon~~
~~await us.~~

poisoned wells

~~Leave these crippled fires~~
~~& blood-stained streets.~~
~~Enter the hot dream,~~
~~Come w/ us.~~
~~Everything is broken up~~
~~& dances.~~

— shhhhhh —

~~Night has arrived~~
w/ her purple legion.
Retire now to your tents
& to your dreams.

Tomorrow we enter
The Town of my birth.

I want to be ready.

|

Music
— —Fade— —
end

|

The lizard and the snake are identified with the unconscious and the forces of evil. That piece "Celebration of the Lizard" was kind of an invitation to the dark forces. It's all done tongue-in-cheek. I don't think people realize that. It's not to be taken seriously. It's like if you play the villain in a western it doesn't mean that that's you. It just an aspect that you keep for show. I don't really take that seriously. That's supposed to be ironic.[7]

Dry Water

The velvet fur of religion
The polish of knife handle & coin
The universe of organic gears
or microscope mechanical
embryo metal doll
The night is a steel machine
grinding its slow stained wheels
The brain is filled w/clocks, & drills
& water down drains
Knife-handle, thick blood
like the coin & cloth
they rub & the skin they love
to touch

the graveyard, the tombstone,
the gloomstone & runestone
The sand & the moon, mating
deep in the Western night
waiting for the escape
of one of our gang
The hangman's noose is a
silver sluice bait
come-on man
your meat is hanging
on the wing of the raven
man's bird, poet's soul

Shhhhhhhhhhhhhhhh
the thin rustle of weeds
the voice comes from faraway
inside, awaiting its birth
in a cool room, on tendril bone
The insane free chummy cackle
of infants in a ballroom, of a
family of friends around
a table, laden w/feast-food
soft guilty female laughter
the bar-room, the men's room
people assemble to establish
armies & find their foe
& fight

.

           Clustered in watchful terror
by vine-growth, the hollow bush
           dry cancerous wells
We awoke before dawn, slipped
           into the canyon

Noon schoolyard screamed
           w/play, the lunch hour ending
ropes & balls slapped hard at
           cement sand, the female land
was bright, all swelling to degree
           most comfortless & guarding

A record noise shot out
           & stunned the earth. The music
had been bolted w/new sound.
           Run, run the end of repose
an anthem has churned
           the bad guys are winning.

           •

Silver shaken in the gloom
I left her

Trees waste & sway forever

Marble porch & sylvan frieze
Down on her knees

She begs the spider-king to wed her
Slides into bed

He turns her over

There is a leather pouch
that's full of silver

It spills like water

She left
And took the coins I gave her

•

As to the drowning man
hoarse whisper
invokes, on the edge,
an arroyo
Sangre de Christo

Violence in a time of plenty

There is one deaf witness
on the bank, the shore
leaning in finery against
a ruined wall
as Jesus did. Red livid lips,
pale flesh withdrawn from
ragged dress, pit of the past
& secrets unveiled in the
scarred chalk wall

When, often, one is not deluged
by rain, 3 drops suffice
The war is over there
I am neither doctor nor saint
Christ or soldier
Now, friends, don't look at me
sadly ranting like some
incomprehensible child
I know by my breath of what
I speak, & what I've seen
needs telling.

Please, freeze!
Danger near.
A message has started its path
to the heart of the brain
A thin signal is on its way

An arrow of hope, predicting rain
A death-rod bearing pain

•

I

I will not come again
I will not come again
into the swirl
The bitter wine-soaked
stallion eats the seed,
all labor is a lie;
no vice is kindled in
these loins to melt
or vie w/any strong
particulating smile.
Leave sundry stones alive.

II

Now that you have gone
all alone
the desert to explore
& left me here alone

the calmness of the town
where a girl in black
gets in a car
& searches numbly
for her keys;

Now that you have gone
or strayed away -

I sit, & listen to the hiss
of traffic & invoke
into this burned & gutted
room some ghost, some
vague resemblance of a time

Off - on, on and off,
like one long sick
electric dream.
This state is confused
state. Out there everyone
is greedy for her love.

They will drain her life
like warm connectors,
plug into her soul
From every side & melt
her form for me.

But I deserve this,
Greatest cannibal of all.
Some tired future.
Let me sleep.
Get on w/the disease.

•

In this dim cave
we can go no further.
Here money is key
to smooth age. Horses,
givers of guilt. Great
bags of gold.

I want obedience!

We examine this ancient
& insane theatre, obscene
like luxuriant churches
altars

I confess
to scarves
cool floors
stroked curtain

The actors are twice-blessed
before us. This is
too serious & severe.

Great mystery!
Timeless passion
patterned in stillness.

•

Sex for you
was thread
which binds
us even now
on this pale
planet.

To the poet
& cover-girl,
photo in color,
to armies
that join,
out on a desert,
& to Samson
& all his
generals
bound quiet
now w/exotic
arch-angels
of dusk, in
Sumarian
& N. African
slumbers.

The bazaar is crowded
as dancers thrive.
Snake-wreaths & pleasures.
I take you to a low cave
called "Calipah".

•

Stand there listening
you will hear them
tiny shapes just beyond
        the moon
Star-flys, jarts,
dismal fronds
stirring ape-jaws striving
to make the morning
mail call

Cry owl.
Hark to the wood-vine.
Suckle-snake crawls, gnawing
restive

I know you.
The one who left to go
warning. Wishless now
& sullen. Transfer
deferred.

Steal me a peach
from the orange tree
grove-keeper

She fell.

What are you doing
w/your hand on her
breast?

She fell, mam.

Give her to me.

Yes, mam.

Go tell the master
what you've done.

They killed him.

Later.

Going up the stairs
handcuffed
to his cell.

A shot-gun blast
Behind the back.

•

I

Untrampled footsteps
Borderline dreams
Occasion for sinners
alive if it seems
given to wander
alone at the shore
wanton to whisper
I am no more
Am as my heart beats
live as I can
wanton to whisper
faraway sands

II

Now come into my pretty isle
My weary westward wanderer
Faraway is as it seems
& so alone shall shelter
Come along unto my sails
as weary islands go
prosper merry as I went
I shall no more the sailor
Shall I ho the sailor

III

Where were you when I needed you?
Where indeed but in some sheltered
Sturdy heaven; wasted, broken
sadly broke & one thin thing to get us thru

IV

Urchin crawl broke
　　　spenders bleeders all
brew North
　　　stained lot
he was lost
　　　out on an aircraft
high above
　　　long awkward brewer's
　　　　　shelters breed

This ugly crew
　　　our poisoned jet
god get us love & get
　　　us speed
To get us home again
　　　love
Crippled by people
　　　cut by nothing
Public housing
　　　the incredible damage
　　　　　can be cured

V

She's my girl friend:
I wouldn't tell her
        Name but I think
you already know her
        Name
            is
Square fire insect
marble saffron intro
demi-rag in flames

it's the same game
whether you call it
by her real name

VI

She lives in the city
        under the sea
Prisoner of pirates
        prisoner of dreams
I want to be w/her
        want her to see
The things I've created
        sea-shells that bleed
Sensitive seeds
        of impossible warships

Dragon-fly hovers
        & wavers & teases
The weeds & his wings
        are in terrible fury
it's time to relieve
            his distress w/drowning[8]

        •

I rely on images of violence, which bring the shock of pain, to penetrate the barriers people erect and defend, not simple defenses; the phony facades people live behind. Blocking their perceptions from coming in, and blocking their feelings from coming out. There are two ways I try to shatter those facades, or at least make a hole where something can get in, to let the trapped feelings out—one way is violence, pain. The other is eroticism.[9]

The New Creatures

I

Snake-skin jacket
Indian eyes
Brilliant hair

He moves in disturbed
Nile Insect
Air

II

You parade thru the soft summer
We watch your eager rifle decay
Your wilderness
Your teeming emptiness
Pale forests on verge of light
decline.

More of your miracles
More of your magic arms

III

Bitter grazing in sick pastures
Animal sadness & the daybed
Whipping.
Iron curtains pried open.
The elaborate sun implies
dust, knives, voices.

Call out of the Wilderness
Call out of fever, receiving
the wet dreams of an Aztec King.

IV

The banks are high & overgrown
rich w/warm green danger.
Unlock the canals.
Punish our sister's sweet playmate distress.
Do you want us that way w/the rest?
Do you adore us?
When you return will you
            still want to play w/us?

V

Fall down.
Strange gods arrive in fast enemy poses.
Their shirts are soft marrying
            cloth & hair together.
All along their arms ornaments
            conceal veins bluer than blood
            pretending welcome.
Soft lizard eyes connect.
Their soft drained insect cries erect
            new fear where fears reign.
The rustling of sex against their skin.
The wind withdraws all sound.
Stamp your witness on the punished ground.

VI

Wounds, stags, & arrows
Hooded flashing legs plunge
            near the tranquil women.
Startling obedience from the pool people
Astonishing caves to plunder.
Loose, nerveless ballets of looting.
Boys are running.
Girls are screaming, falling.
The air is thick w/smoke.
Dead crackling wires dance pools
            of sea blood.

VII

Lizard woman
w/your insect eyes
w/your wild surprise.
Warm daughter of silence.
Venom.
Turn your back w/a slither of moaning wisdom.
The unblinking blind eyes
        behind walls new histories rise,
and wake growling & shining
        the weird dawn of dreams.
Dogs lie sleeping.
The wolf howls.
A creature lives out the war.
A forest.
A rustle of cut words, choking
river.

VIII

The snake, the lizard, the insect eye
the huntsman's green obedience.
Quick, in raw time, serving
        stealth & slumber,
grinding warm forests into restless lumber.

Now for the valley.
Now for the syrup hair.
Stabbing the eyes, widening skies
behind the skull bone.
Swift end of hunting.
Hug round the swollen torn breast
        & red-stained throat.
The hounds gloat.
Take her home.
Carry our sister's body, back
to the boat.

        •

A pair of Wings
Crash
High winds of Karma

Sirens

Laughter & young voices
in the mts.

　　　•

Saints
the Negro, Africa
Tattoo
　　　eyes like time

　　　•

Build temporary habitations, games
& chambers, play there, hide.

First man stood, shifting stance
while germs of sight
unfurl'd Flags in his skull

and quickening, hair, nails, skin
turned slowly, whirl'd, in
the warm aquarium, warm
wheel turning.

Cave fish, eels, & gray salamanders
turn in their night career of sleep.

The idea of vision escapes
the animal worm whose earth
is an ocean, whose eye is its body.

　　　•

The theory is that birth is prompted
by the child's desire to leave the womb.
But in the photograph an unborn horse's
neck strains inward w/legs scooped out.

From this everything follows:

Swallow milk at the breast
until there's no milk.

Squeeze wealth at the rim
Until tile pools claim it.

He swallows seed, his pride
until w/pale mouth legs

she sucks the root, dreading
world to devour child.

Doesn't the ground swallow me
when I die, or the sea
if I die at sea?

•

The City. Hive, Web, or severed
insect mound. All citizens heirs
of the same royal parent.

The caged beast, the holy centre,
a garden in the midst of the city.

> "See Naples & die."
> Jump ship. Rats, sailors
> & death.

> So many wild pigeons.
> Animals ripe w/new diseases.
> "There is only one disease
> and I am its catalyst,"
> cried doomed pride of the carrier.

> Fighting, dancing, gambling,
> bars, cinemas thrive
> in the avid summer.

•

Savage destiny

Naked girl, seen from behind,
on a natural road

Friends
explore the labyrinth

- - Movie
    young woman left on the desert

A city gone mad w/fever

     •

Sisters of the unicorn, dance
Sisters & brothers of Pyramid
Dance

Mangled hands
Tales of the Old Days
Discovery of the Sacred Pool
changes
Mute-handed stillness baby cry

The wild dog
The sacred beast

Find her!

     •

He goes to see the girl
of the ghetto
Dark savage streets.
A hut, lighted by candle.
She is magician
Female prophet
Sorceress
Dressed in the past
All arrayed.

The stars
The moon
She reads the future
in your hand

•

The walls are garish red
The stairs
High discordant screaming
She has the tokens.
"You too"
"Don't go"
He flees.
Music renews.

The mating-pit.
'Salvation'
Tempted to leap in circle.

Negroes riot.

•

Fear the Lords who are secret among us.
The Lords are w/in us.
Born of sloth & cowardice.

•

He spoke to me. He frightened
me w/laughter. He took
my hand, & led me past
silence into cool whispered
Bells.

•

A file of young people
going thru a small woods

●

They are filming something
in the street, in front of
our house.

●

Walking to the riot
Spreads to the houses
the lawns
     suddenly alive now
     w/people
     running

●

I don't dig what they did
to that girl
Mercy pack
Wild song they sing
As they chop her hands
Nailed to a ghost
Tree

I saw a lynching
Met the strange men
     of the southern swamp
Cypress was their talk
Fish-call & bird-song
Roots & signs
     out of all knowing
They chanced to be there
Guides, to the white
gods.

●

An armed camp.
Army army
burning itself in
feasts

•

Jackal, we sniff after the survivors of caravans
We reap bloody crops on war fields.
No meat of any corpse deprives our lean bellies.
Hunger drives us on scented winds
Stranger, traveller,
peer into our eyes & translate
the horrible barking of ancient dogs.

•

Camel caravans bear
Witness guns to Caesar.
Hordes crawl & seep inside
the walls. The streets
flow stone. Life goes
on absorbing war. Violence
kills the temple of no sex.

•

Terrible shouts start
            the journey
-- If they had migrated sooner

-- a high wailing keening
   piercing animal lament
   from a woman
   High atop a Mt. tower

-- Thin wire fence
in the mind
dividing the heart

•

Surreptitiously
They smile
Inviting -- Smiling

    Choktai
    leave!
    evil
    leave!
    No come here
    Leave her!

A creature is nursing
its child
soft arms around
the head & the neck
a mouth to connect
leave this child alone
This one is mine
I'm taking her home
Back to the rain

    •

The assassin's bullet
Marries the King
Dissembling miles of air
To kiss the crown.

The Prince rambles in blood.
Ode to the neck
That was groomed
For rape's gown.

    •

Cancer city
Urban fall
Summer sadness
The highways of the old town
Ghosts in cars
Electric shadows

    •

Ensenada
the dead seal
the dog crucifix
ghosts of the dead car sun.
Stop the car.
Rain. Night.
Feel.

    •

Sea-bird sea-moan
Earthquake murmuring
Fast-burning incense
Clamoring surging
Serpentine road
To the chinese caves
Home of the winds
The gods of mourning

    •

The city sleeps
& the unhappy children
roam w/animal gangs
They seem to speak
to their friends
the dogs
who teach them trails.
Who can catch them?
Who can make them come
inside?

    •

The tent girl
at midnight
stole to the well
& met her lover there
They talked a while
& laughed
& then he left
She put an orange pillow
on her breast

In the morning
Chief w/drew his troops
Explained a map
The horsemen rose on up
the women fixed the ropes
on tight
the tents are folded now
we march toward the sea

•

Catalog of Horrors
Descriptions of Natural disaster
Lists of miracles in the divine corridor
Catalog of fish in the divine canal
Catalog of objects in the room
List of things in the sacred river

•

I

The soft parade has now begun
on Sunset.
Cars come thundering down
the canyon.
Now is the time & the place.
The cars come rumbling.
"You got a cool machine."
These engine beasts
muttering their soft
talk. A delight
at night
to hear their quiet voices
again
after 2 years.
Now the soft parade
has soon begun.
cool pools
from a tired land
sink now
in the peace of evening.
clouds weaken
& die.
The sun, an orange skull,
whispers quietly, becomes an
island, & is gone.

There they are
watching
us everything
will be dark.
The light changed.
We were aware
knee-deep in the fluttering air
as the ships move on
trains in their wake.
Trench mouth
again in the camps.
Gonorrhea
Tell the girl to go home
We need a witness
to the killing.

II

The artists of Hell
set up easels in parks
the terrible landscape,
where citizens find anxious pleasure
preyed upon by savage bands of youths
I can't believe this is happening
I can't believe all these people
are sniffing each other
& backing away
teeth grinning
hair raised, growling, here in
the slaughtered wind

I am ghost killer.
witnessing to all
my blessed sanction
This is it
no more fun
the death of all joy
has come.

Do you dare
deny my
potency
my kindness
or forgiveness?

Just try
you will fry
like the rest
in holiness
And not for a
penny
will I spare
any time
for you
Ghost children
down there
in the frightening world

You are alone
& have no need of other
you & the child mother

who bore you
who weaned you
who made you man

III

Photo-booth killer
fragile bandit
straight from ambush
Kill me!
Kill the child who made
Thee.
Kill the thought-provoking
senator of lust
who brought you to this state.
Kill hate
disease
warfare
sadness
Kill badness
Kill madness
Kill photo mother murder tree
Kill me.
Kill yourself
Kill the little blind elf.

•

The beautiful monster
vomits a stream of watches
clocks jewels knives silver
coins & copper blood

The well of time & trouble
whiskey bottles perfume
razor blades beads
liquid insects hammers
& thin nails the feet of
birds eagle feather & claws
machine parts chrome
teeth hair shards of
pottery & skulls the ruins
of our time the debris by
a lake the gleaming
beer cans & rust & sable
menstrual fur

Dance naked on broken
bones feet bleed & stain
glass cuts cover your mind
& the dry end of vacuum
boat while the people
drop lines in still pools
& pull ancient trout
from the deep home. Scales
crusted & gleaming green
A knife was stolen. A
valuable hunting knife
By some strange boys
from the other camp across
the Lake

•

I

Are these our friends
racing & shuddering
thru the calm vales of parliament

My son will not die in the war
He will return
numbed peasant voice of orient
fisherman

Last time you said
this was the only way
voice of tender young girl

Running & speaking
infected green
jungles

consult the oracle

bitter creek
crawl
they exist on rainwater

monkey-love
mantra mate
maker of brandy

The poison isles
The poison
Take this thin granule
of evil snakeroot

from the southern
shore

way out miracle
will find thee

The chopper blazed over
inward click & sure
blasted matter, made
the time-bombs free

of leprous lands
spotted w/hunger
& clinging to law
Please
show us your ragged head
& silted smiling eyes
calm in fire

a silky flowered shirt
edging the eyes, alive
spidery, distant
dial lies

come, calm one
into the life-try

already wife-like
latent, leathery, loose
lawless, large & languid

She was a kingdom-cry
legion of lewd marching
mind-men

Where are your manners
out there on the sunlit
desert

boundless galaxies of dust
cactus spines, beads
bleach stones, bottles
& rust cars, stored for shaping

The new man, time-soldier
picked his way narrowly
thru the crowded ruins
of once grave city, gone
comic now w/rats
& the insects of refuge

He lives in cars
goes fruitless thru
the frozen schools
& finds no space

in shades of obedience
The monitors are silenced
the great graveled guard-towers
sicken on the westward beach
so tired of watching

if only one horse were left
to ride thru the waste
a dog at his side
to sniff meat-maids
chained on the public poles

there is no more argument
in beds, at night
blackness is burned

Stare into the parlors of town
where a woman dances
in her european gown
to the great waltzes

this could be fun
to rule a wasteland

II

Cherry palms
Terrible shores
& more
& many more
This we know
that all are free
in the school-made
text of the unforgiven

deceit smiles
incredible hardships are suffered
by those barely able
to endure

but all will pass
lie down in green grass
& smile, & muse, & gaze

 upon her smooth
resemblance
to the mating-Queen
who it seems
is in love
w/the horseman

now, isn't that fragrant
Sir, isn't that knowing
w/a wayward careless
backward glance

July 24, 1968
Los Angeles, The United States, Hawaii[10]

When I wrote "The New Creatures,"
I was very naïve. It wasn't something that
was born out of any great awareness of
the universe. It's a very naïve little book,
but somehow a lot of it holds up.

I had a book on lizards and snakes and
reptiles and the first sentence of it struck
me acutely—"reptiles are the interesting
descendants of magnificent ancestors."
Another thing about them is that they are
a complete anachronism. If every reptile
in the world were to disappear tomorrow,
it wouldn't really change the balance
of nature one bit. They are a completely
arbitrary species.[11]

THE LORDS
Notes on Vision

JAMES DOUGLAS MORRISON

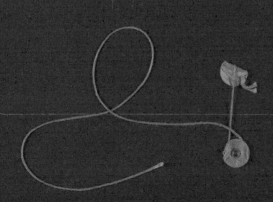

The Lords/Notes on Vision

Look where we worship.

•

"Players" - the child, the actor, and the gambler.
The idea of chance is absent from the world of the
child and primitive. The gambler also feels in
service of an alien power. Chance is a survival
of religion in the modern city, as is theatre,
more often cinema, the religion of possession.

•

When men conceived buildings,
and closed themselves in chambers,
first trees and caves.

(Windows work two ways,
mirrors one way.)

You never walk through mirrors
or swim through windows.

•

The bird or insect that stumbles into a room,
and cannot find the window. Because they know
no 'windows.'

Wasps, poised in the window
Excellent dancers
Detached, are not inclined
Into our chamber.

room of withering mesh
Read love's vocabulary
In the green lamp
of tumescent flesh.

•

Kynaston's bride
may not appear
But the odor of her flesh
is never very far.

•

Crisp hot whiteness
City Noon
Occupants of plague zone
are consumed.

(Santa Ana's are winds off deserts.)

Rip up grating and splash in gutters.
the search for water, moisture,
'Wetness' of the actor, lover.

•

Not one of the prisoners regained sexual balance.
Depressions, impotency, sleeplessness . . . erotic
dispersions in languages, reading, games, music,
and gymnastics.

The prisoners built their own theatre which
testified to an incredible surfeit of leisure.
A young sailor, forced into female roles, soon
became the 'town' darling, for by this time they
called themselves a town, and elected a mayor,
police, aldermen.

•

Sleep is an under-ocean dipped into each night.
At morning, awake dripping, gasping, eyes
stinging.

•

The 'stranger' was sensed as greatest menace
in ancient communities.

•

The voyeur is masturbator, the mirror his badge,
the window his prey.

•

Male genitals are small faces
forming trinities of thieves
and Christs
Fathers, sons, and ghosts.

A nose hangs over a wall
And two half eyes, sad eyes,
Mute and handless, multiply
an endless round of victories.

These dry and secret triumphs, fought
in stalls and stamped in prisons,
glorify our walls
and scorch our vision.

A horror of empty spaces
Propagates this seal on private places.

•

It is wrong to assume, as some have done, that
cinema belongs to women. Cinema is created by
men for the consolation of men.

•

The shadow plays originally were restricted to
male audiences. Men could view these dream shows
from either side of the screen. When women later
began to be admitted, they were allowed to attend
only to shadows.

•

The modern East creates the greatest body of films.
Cinema is a new form of an ancient tradition - the
shadow play. Even their theatre is an imitation
of it. Born in India or China, the shadow show
was aligned with religious ritual, linked with
celebrations which centered around cremation of the
dead.

•

The appeal of cinema lies in the fear of death.

•

When play dies it becomes the Game.
When sex dies it becomes Climax.

•

In the womb we are blind cave fish.

•

Surround Emperor of Body.
Bali Bali dancers
Will not break my temple.

Explorers
Suck eyes into the head.

The rosy body cross
secret in flow
controls its flow.

Wrestlers
in body weights dance
& music, mimesis, body

Swimmers
Entertain embryo
Sweet dangerous thrust flow.

•

In Rome, prostitutes were exhibited on roofs
above the public highways for the dubious
hygiene of loose tides of men whose potential
lust endangered the fragile order of power.
It is even reported that patrician ladies, masked
and naked, sometimes offered themselves up to
these deprived eyes for private excitements of
their own.

·

Modern circles of Hell: Oswald (?) kills President.
Oswald enters taxi. Oswald stops at rooming house.
Oswald leaves taxi. Oswald kills officer Tippit.
Oswald sheds jacket. Oswald is captured.

He escaped into a movie house.

·

The subject says "I see first lots of things
which dance . . . then everything becomes gradually
connected."

·

Strange, fertile correspondences the alchemists
sensed in unlikely orders of being. Between
men and planets, plants and gestures, words and
weather. These disturbing connections: an infant's cry and the stroke of silk; the whorl
of an ear and an appearance of dogs in the yard;
a woman's head lowered in sleep and the morning
dance of cannibals, these are conjunctions which
transcend the sterile signal of any 'willed'
montage. These juxtapositions of objects, sounds,
actions, colors, weapons, wounds, and odors shine
in an unheard of way, impossible ways.

Film is nothing when not an illumination of
this chain of being which makes a needle poised
in flesh call up explosions in a foreign capital.

·

Objects as they exist in time the clean eye and
camera give us. Not falsified by 'seeing.'

                    •

Metamorphose. An object is cut off from its name,
habits, associations. Detached, it becomes only
the thing, in and of itself. When this disintegration
into pure existence is at last achieved, the object
is free to become endlessly anything.

                    •

Muybridge derived his animal subjects from the
Philadelphia Zoological Garden, male performers
from the University. The women were professional
artists' models, also actresses and dancers,
parading nude before the 48 cameras.

                    •

Film confers a kind of spurious eternity.

                    •

Robert Baker, an Edinburgh artist, while in jail
for debt, was struck by the effect of light shining
through the bars of his cell through a letter he
was reading, and out of this perception he invented the first *Panorama*, a concave, transparent
picture view of the city.

This invention was soon replaced by the *Diorama*
which added the illusion of movement by shifting
the room. Also sounds and novel lighting effects.
Daguerre's London Diorama still stands in Regent
Park, a rare survival, since these shows depended
always on effects of artificial light, produced
by lamps or gas jets, and nearly always ended
in fire.

                    •

In 1832, Gropius was astounding Paris with his Pleorama. The audience was transformed into the crew aboard a ship engaged in battle. Fire, screaming, sailors, drowning.

•

When there are as yet no objects.

•

Phantasmagoria, magic-lantern shows, spectacles without substance. They achieved complete sensory experiences through noise, incense, lightning, water. There may be a time when we'll attend Weather Theatres to recall the sensation of rain.

•

Cinema has evolved in two paths.

One is spectacle. Like the Phantasmagoria, its goal is the creation of a total substitute sensory world.

The other is peep show, which claims for its realm both the erotic and the untampered observance of real life, and imitates the keyhole or voyeur's window without need of color, noise, grandeur.

•

Cinema is most totalitarian of the arts. All energy and sensation is sucked up into the skull, a cerebral erection, skull bloated with blood. Caligula wished a single neck for all his subjects that he could behead a kingdom with one blow. Cinema is this transforming agent. The body exists for the sake of the eyes; it becomes a dry stalk to support these two soft insatiable jewels.

•

Cinema returns us to anima, religion of matter,
which gives each thing its special divinity and
sees gods in all things and beings.

Cinema, heir of alchemy, last of an erotic science.

•

The alchemists detected in the sexual activity of
man a correspondence with the world's creation,
with the growth of plants and with mineral
formations. When they saw the union of rain
and earth, they saw it in an erotic sense, as
copulation. And this extended to all natural
realms of matter. For they could picture love
affairs of chemicals & stars, a romance of
stones, or the fertility of fire.

•

Few would defend a small view of Alchemy as 'Mother
of Chemistry', and confuse its true goal with those
external metal arts. Alchemy is an erotic science,
involved in buried aspects of reality, aimed
at purifying and transforming all being and matter.
Not to suggest that material operations are ever
abandoned. The adept holds both the mystical
and physical work.

•

A drunken crowd knocked over the apparatus,
and Mayhew's showman, exhibiting at Islington
Green, burned up, with his mate, inside.

•

Today the doors of all projection booths are made
of steel.

Does the theatre keep out light, or keep in darkness?

•

Baths, bars, the indoor pool. Our injured leader
prone on the sweating tile. Chlorine on his breath
and in his long hair. Lithe, although crippled,
body of a middle-weight contender. Near him
and trusted journalist, confidante. He liked men
near him with a large sense of life. But most
of the press were vultures descending on the
scene for curious America aplomb. Cameras
inside the coffin interviewing worms.

•

Camera, as all-seeing god, satisfies our longing
for omniscience. To spy on others from this
height and angle: pedestrians pass in and out of
our lens like rare aquatic insects.

•

Yoga powers. To make oneself invisible or small.
To become gigantic and reach to the farthest things.
To change the course of nature. To place oneself
anywhere in space or time. To summon the dead.
To exalt senses and perceive inaccessible images,
of events on other worlds, in one's deepest inner
mind, or in the minds of others.

•

The sniper's rifle is an extension of his eye. He
kills with injurious vision.

•

It takes large murder to turn rocks in the shade
and expose strange worms beneath. The lives of
our discontented madmen are revealed.

•

The assassin (?), in flight, gravitated with
unconscious, instinctual insect ease, moth-
like, toward a zone of safety, haven from the
swarming streets. Quickly, he was devoured
in the warm, dark, silent maw of the physical
theatre.

·

Inside the dream, button sleep around your body
like a glove. Free now of space and time. Free
to dissolve in the streaming summer.

·

Novices, we watch the moves of silkworms who excite
their bodies in moist leaves & weave wet nests
of hair & skin.

This is a model of our liquid resting world
Dissolving bone and melting marrow
Opening pores as wide as windows.

·

The eye looks vulgar
Inside its ugly shell
Come out in the open
In all of your Brilliance.

·

Nothing. The air outside
Burns my eyes.
I'll pull them out
and get rid of the burning.

•

All games contain the idea of death.

•

On the third of January, near the door of his
lodgings, Nietzsche saw a cabman whipping a
horse. He threw his arms around the animal's
neck and burst into tears, marking first hour
of his madness.

He purposely contracted syphilis as a student -
playing Wagner on an upright for the whores - and
carried the germs of chaos all his years. When he
at last despaired of embodying in words his
entire world of thought, he let those forces
sweep through him and explode chambers in his
brain.

But not before capping his philosophy with that
last symbolic act - the final chapter in his
philosophy - and wed himself with the act and
animal for all time.

•

The happening/the event in which ether is introduced
into a roomful of people through air vents makes
the chemical an actor. Its agent, or injector,
is an artist-showman who creates a performance to witness
himself. The people consider themselves
audience, while they perform for each other,
and the gas acts out poems of its own through
the medium of the human body. This approaches
the psychology of the orgy while remaining in
the realm of the Game and its infinite permutations.

The aim of the happening is to cure boredom,
wash the eyes, make child-like reconnections
with the stream of life. Its lowest, widest
aim is for purgation of perception. The happening
attempts to engage all the senses, the total
organism, and achieve total response in the face of
traditional arts which focus on narrower inlets
of sensation.

Multi-medias are invariably sad comedies. They
work as a kind of colorful group therapy, a
woeful mating of actors and viewers, a mutual
semi-masturbation. The performers seem to need
their audience and the spectators - the spectators
would find these same mild titillations in a freak
show or fun Fair and fancier, more complete
amusements in a Mexican cathouse.

.

June 30th. On the sun roof. He woke up suddenly.
At that instant a jet from the air base crawled
in silence overhead. On the beach, children try
to leap into its swift shadow.

.

Destroy roofs, walls, see in all the rooms at once.

From the air we trapped gods, with the gods
omniscient gaze, but without their power to be
inside minds and cities as they fly above.

.

Everything is vague and dizzy. The skin swells and
there is no more distinction between parts of the
body. An encroaching sound of threatening,
mocking, monotonous voices. This is fear and
attraction of being swallowed.

·

Imagery is born of loss. Loss of the 'friendly
expanses.' The breast is removed and the face
imposes its cold, curious, forceful, and inscrutable
presence.

·

You may enjoy life from afar. You may look at
things but not taste them. You may caress
the mother only with the eyes.

·

A room moves over a landscape, uprooting the mind,
astonishing vision. A grey film melts off the
eyes, and runs down the cheeks. Farewell.

Modern life is a journey by car. The Passengers
change terribly in their reeking seats, or roam
from car to car, subject to unceasing transformation.
Inevitable progress is made toward the beginning
(there is no difference in terminals), as we
slice through cities, whose ripped backsides present
a moving picture of windows, signs, streets,
buildings. Sometimes other vessels, closed
worlds, vacuums, travel along beside to move
ahead or fall utterly behind.

·

Films are collections of dead pictures which are
given artificial insemination.

·

It is wrong to assume that art needs the spectator
in order to be. The films runs on without any eyes.
The spectator cannot exist without it. It insures
his existence.

•

Each film depends upon all the others, and drives
you on to others. Cinema was a novelty, a scienti-
fic toy, until a sufficient body of works had been
amassed, enough to create an intermittent other
world, a powerful, infinite mythology to be dipped
into at will.

Films have an illusion of timelessness fostered
by their regular, indomitable appearance.

•

You cannot touch these phantoms.

•

Cinema discovers its fondest affinities, not
with painting, literature, or theatre, but with
the popular diversions - comics, chess, French
and Tarot decks, magazines, and tattooing.

•

Cinema derives not from painting, literature,
sculpture, theatre, but from ancient popular
wizardry. It is the contemporary manifestation
of an evolving history of shadows, a delight in
pictures that move, a belief in magic. Its
lineage is entwined from the earliest beginning
with Priests and sorcery, a summoning of phantoms.
With, at first, only slight aid of the mirror and
fire, men called up dark and secret visits from
regions in the buried mind. In these seances,
shapes are spirits which ward off evil.

•

Film spectators are quiet vampires.

•

The voyeur, the peeper, the Peeping Tom, is a dark
comedian. He is repulsive in his dark anonymity,
in his secret invasion. He is pitifully alone.
But, strangely, he is able through this same silence
and concealment to make unknowing partner of anyone
within his eye's range. This is his threat and
power.

•

There are no glass houses. The shades are drawn
and 'real' life begins. Some activities are impossible
in the open. And these secret events are the voyeur's
game. He seeks them out with his myriad army of
eyes - like the child's notion of a Deity who sees
all. "Everything?" asks the child. "Yes, everything" they answer, and the child is left to cope
with this divine intrusion.

•

Early film-makers, who - like the alchemists -
delighted in a willful obscurity about their craft,
in order to withhold their skills from profane
onlookers.

•

Separate, purify, reunite. The formula of
Ars Magna, and its heir, the cinema.

•

The camera is an androgynous machine, a kind of
mechanical hermaphrodite.

•

Cure blindness with a whore's spittle.

•

In his retort the alchemist repeats the work of
Nature.

•

Urge to come to terms with the "Outside," by
absorbing, interiorizing it. I won't come out,
you must come in to me. Into my womb-garden
where I peer out. Where I can construct a universe
within the skull, to rival the real.

·

More or less, we're all afflicted with the psychology
of the voyeur. Not in a strictly clinical or
criminal sense, but in our whole physical and emotional
stance before the world. Whenever we seek to break
this spell of passivity, our actions are cruel and
awkward and generally obscene, like an invalid who
has forgotten how to walk.

·

The Andalusian Bitch. What does it mean? The
artist's own hand slits her eyeball. Cloud razors
slash at the moon. Cosmic utterance. He has
lanced the swollen boil of sight.

·

A mild possession, devoid of risk, at bottom
sterile. With an image there is no attendant
danger.

·

She said "Your eyes are always black." The pupil
opens to seize the object of vision.

·

French Deck. Solitary stroker of cards. He
dealt himself a hand. Turn stills of the past in
unending permutations, shuffle and begin. Sort
the images again. And sort them again. This
game reveals germs of truth, and death.

·

The world becomes an apparently infinite, yet
possibly finite, card game. Image combinations,
permutations, comprise the world game.

●

We all live in the city.

The City forms - often physically, but inevitably
psychically - a circle. A Game. A ring of death
with sex at its center. Drive toward outskirts
of city suburbs. At the edge discover zones of
sophisticated vice and boredom, child prosti-
tution. But in the grimy ring immediately surrounding the daylight business district exists the only
real crowd life of our mound, the only street
life, nightlife. Diseased specimens in dollar
hotels, low boarding houses, bars, pawn shops,
burlesques and brothels, in dying arcades which
never die, in streets and streets of all-night
cinemas.

●

What sacrifice, at what price can the city be born?

●

The spectator is a dying animal.

●

Through ventriloquism, gestures, play with objects,
and all rare variations of the body in space,
the shaman signalled his 'trip' to an audience
which shared the journey.

●

Invoke, palliate, drive away the Dead. Nightly.

●

Principle of seance: to cure illness. A mood
might overtake a people burdened by historical
events or dying in a bad landscape. They seek
deliverance from doom, death, dread. Seek possession, the visit of gods and powers, a re-winning
of the life-source from demon possessors. The
cure is culled from ecstasy. Cure illness or
prevent its visit, revive the sick, and regain
stolen, soul.

•

In the seance, the shaman led. A sensuous panic,
deliberately evoked through drugs, chants, dancing,
hurls the shaman into trance. Changed voice,
convulsive movement. He acts like a madman. These
professional hysterics, chosen precisely for their
psychotic leaning, were once esteemed. They
mediated between man and spirit-world. Their mental
travels formed the crux of the religious life of
the tribe.

•

In old Russia, the Czar, each year, granted -
out of the shrewdness of his own soul or one of
his advisors - a week's freedom for one convict
in each of his prisons. The choice was left to the
prisoners themselves and it was determined in
several ways. Sometimes by vote, sometimes by lot,
often by force. It was apparent that the chosen
must be a man of magic, virility, experience,
perhaps narrative skill, a man of possibility, in
short, a hero. Impossible situation at the
moment of freedom, impossible selection,
defining our world in its percussions.

•

I. POEMS AND WRITINGS

The Lords. Events take place beyond our knowledge
or control. Our lives are lived for us. We can
only try to enslave others. But gradually, special
perceptions are being developed. The idea of the
'Lords' is beginning to form in some minds. We
should enlist them into bands of perceivers to
tour the labyrinth during their mysterious noc-
turnal appearances. The Lords have secret entrances,
and they know disguises. But they give themselves
away in minor ways. Too much glint of light in
the eye. A wrong gesture. Too long and curious a
glance.

The Lords appease us with images. They give us
books, concerts, galleries, shows, cinemas. Especially the cinemas. Through art they confuse
us and blind us to our enslavement. Art adorns
our prison walls, keeps us silent and diverted
and indifferent.

•

There are no longer 'dancers,' the possessed.
The cleavage of men into actor and spectators
is the central fact of our time. We are obsessed
with heroes who live for us and whom we punish.
If all the radios and televisions were deprived
of their sources of power, all books and paintings
burned tomorrow, all shows and cinemas closed,
all the arts of vicarious existence . . .

We are content with the 'given' in sensation's
quest. We have been metamorphosised from a mad
body dancing on hillsides, to a pair of eyes
staring in the dark.

•

Dull lions prone on a watery beach.
The universe kneels at the swamp
To curiously eye its own raw
                        postures of decay
in the mirror of human consciousness.

Absent and peopled mirror, absorbent,
passive to whatever visits
and retains its interest.

Door of passage to the other side,
The soul frees itself in stride.

Turn mirrors to the wall
in the house of the new dead[12]

I did most of "The Lords" when I was at the film school at UCLA. It was really a thesis on film aesthetics. I wasn't able to make films then, so all I was able to do was think about them and write about them and it probably reflects a lot of that. A lot of passages in it, for example, about shamanism turned out to be very prophetic several years later because I had no idea when I was writing that I'd be doing just that.

What "The Lords" is a lot about is the feeling of powerlessness and helplessness that people have in the face of reality. They have no real control over events or their own lives. Something is controlling them. The closest they ever get is the television set.

In creating this idea of "The Lords" it also came to reverse itself. Now, to me, "The Lords" means something entirely different. I couldn't really explain. It's like the opposite. Somehow the Lords are a romantic race of people who have found a way to control their environment and their own lives. They're somehow different from other people.[13]

AN AMERICAN PRAYER

JIM MORRISON

An American Prayer

Do you know the warm progress
                          under the stars?
Do you know we exist?
Have you forgotten the keys
          to the Kingdom?
Have you been borne yet
                      & are you alive?

Let's reinvent the gods, all the myths
                        of the ages
Celebrate symbols from deep elder forests
[Have you forgotten the lessons
                     of the ancient war]

We need great golden copulations

The fathers are cackling in trees of the forest
Our mother is dead in the sea

Do you know we are being led to
         slaughters by placid admirals
& that fat slow generals are getting
         obscene on young blood

Do you know we are ruled by T.V.
The moon is a dry blood beast
Guerrilla bands are rolling numbers
         in the next block of green vine
amassing for warfare on innocent herdsmen
         who are just dying

O great creator of being
grant us one more hour to
         perform our art
         & perfect our lives

The moths & atheists are doubly divine
         & dying
We live, we die
& death not ends it
Journey we more into the
   Nightmare

Cling to life
     our passion'd flower
Cling to cunts & cocks
     of despair
We got our final vision
     by clap
Columbus' groin got
                    filled w/green death

               (I touched her thigh
     & death smiled)

We have assembled inside this ancient
     & insane theatre
To propagate our lust for life
     & flee the swarming wisdom
                    of the streets

The barns are stormed
The windows kept
& only one of all the rest
To dance & save us
W/the divine mockery
     of words
Music inflames temperament

(When the true King's murderers
   are allowed to roam free
     a 1000 Magicians arise
        in the land)

Where are the feasts
we were promised
Where is the wine
   The New Wine
        (dying on the vine)

resident mockery
give us an hour for magic
We of the purple glove
We of the starling flight
        & velvet hour
We of arabic pleasure's breed
We of sundome & the night

Give us a creed
To believe
A night of Lust
Give us trust in
The Night

Give of color
hundred hues
a rich Mandala
for me & you

& for your silky
pillowed house
a head, wisdom
& a bed

Troubled decree
Resident mockery
has claimed thee

We used to believe
in the good old days
We still receive
In little ways

The Things of Kindness
& unsporting brow
Forget & allow

Did you know freedom exists
    in a school book
Did you know madmen are
    running our prison
w/in a jail, w/in a gaol
w/in a white free protestant
maelstrom

We're perched headlong
    on the edge of boredom
We're reaching for death
    on the end of a candle
We're trying for something
    That's already found us

We can invent Kingdoms of our own
grand purple thrones, those chairs of lust
& love we must, in beds of rust

Steel doors lock in prisoner's screams
& muzak, AM, rocks their dreams
No black men's pride to hoist the beams
while mocking angels sift what seems

To be a collage of magazine dust
Scratched on foreheads of walls of trust
This is just jail for those who must
get up in the morning & fight for such

unusable standards
while weeping maidens
show-off penury & pout
ravings for a mad
staff

Wow, I'm sick of doubt
Live in the light of certain
South

Cruel bindings
The servants have the power
dog-men & their mean women
pulling poor blankets over
our sailors
            (& where were you in our lean hour)

Milking your moustache?
or grinding a flower?
I'm sick of dour faces
Staring at me from the T.V.
Tower. I want roses in
my garden bower; dig?

Royal babies, rubies
must now replace aborted
Strangers in the mud
These mutants, blood-meal
for the plant that's plowed

They are waiting to take us into
        the severed garden
Do you know how pale & wanton thrillful
            comes death on a strange hour
            unannounced, unplanned for
like a scaring over-friendly guest you've
        brought to bed

Death makes angels of us all
        & gives us wings
where we had shoulders
        smooth as raven's
                claws

No more money, no more fancy dress
This other Kingdom seems by far the best
until its other jaw reveals incest
& loose obedience to a vegetable law

I will not go
Prefer a Feast of Friends
To the Giant family

II

Great screaming Christ
Upsy-daisy
Lazy Mary will you get up
upon a Sunday morning

"The movie will begin in 5 moments"
The mindless Voice announced
"All those unseated, will await
The next show"

We filed slowly, languidly
into the hall. The auditorium
was vast, & silent.
As we seated & were darkened

The Voice continued:

"The program for this evening
is not new. You have seen
This entertainment thru & thru.
You've seen your birth, your
life & death; you might recall
all of the rest - (did you
have a good world when you
died?) - enough to base
a movie on?"

An iron chuckle rapped our
minds like a fist.

I'm getting out of here
Where're you going?
To the other side of morning
Please don't chase the clouds
pagodas, temples

Her cunt gripped him
like a warm friendly
hand.

"It's all right.
All your friends are here."

When can I meet them?
"After you've eaten"
I'm not hungry
"O, we meant beaten"

Silver stream, silvery scream,
impossible concentration

Here come the comedians
look at them smile
Watch them dance
an indian mile

Look at them gesture
How aplomb
So to gesture everyone

Words dissemble
Words be quick
Words resemble walking sticks

Plant them
They will grow
Watch them waver so

I'll always be
a word-man
Better than a birdman

But I'll charge
Won't get away
w/out lodging a dollar

Shall I say it again
aloud, you get the point
No food w/out fuel's gain

I'll be, the irish loud
unleashed my beak
at peak of powers

O girl, unleash
your worried comb

O worried mind

Sin in the fallen
Backwoods by the blind

She smells debt
on my new collar

Arrogant prose
Tied in a network of fast quest
Hence the obsession

Its quick to admit
Fast borrowed rhythm
Woman came between them

Women of the world unite
Make the world safe
For a scandalous life

Hee Heee
Cut your throat
Life is a joke

Your wife's in a moat
The same boat
Here comes the goat

Blood Blood Blood Blood
They're making a joke
of our universe

III

Matchbox
Are you more real than me
I'll burn you, & set you free
Wept bitter tears
Excessive courtesy
I won't forget

IV

A hot sick lava flowed up,
Rustling & bubbling.   The idiot took
his mind off his flowers, calling
robins doee.   Neat marshall
of enterprise.   Thought fall diamond.
You wouldn't know class - if it fell
on your ass.   Indeed.   Motel
Swimming pool.
Ass high in junk.   The paper face.
Mirror-mask, I love you mirror.
Venetian blinds.   Mediterranean
Trot.   Trout-fishing.   What's for
lunch.
Index
of Pool (comfort chair, rod [aluminum]
peel, tan, orange flavor golf ball)
Hit his head on a Texas green
                    "ya wanta fight"
hard gloves, worthy of sinners fight
    clean
a hard win

He had been brainwashed for 4 hrs.
The Lt. puzzled in again
  "ready to talk"
No sir - was all he'd say.
    Go back to the gym.
    Very peaceful
    Meditation

Shower (of conVenience)
a military station in the desert
looking out venetian blinds
a plane
a desert flower
movie air base
cool cartoon

The rest of the world (?) Travel proving
is reckless & dangerous
Look at the cartoons
of brothels
Stag films

The ship leaves port
EXPLORATION

V

A ship leaves port
mean horse of another thicket
wishbone of desire
decry the metal fox[14]

If you run into some good luck and you get some money, then I think you should just keep pouring it back into creative ventures. Don't go out and buy a bunch of diamond rings and stuff, pour it back into creative ventures.[15]

Ode to LA while thinking of Brian Jones, Deceased

I'm a resident of a city
They've just picked me to play
the Prince of Denmark

Poor Ophelia

All those ghosts he never saw
Floating to doom
On an iron candle

Come back, brave warrior
Do the dive
On another channel

Hot buttered pool
Where's Marrakesh
Under the falls
the wild storm
where savages fell out
in late afternoon
monsters of rhythm

You've left your
Nothing
to compete w/
Silence

I hope you went out
Smiling
Like a child
Into the cool remnant
of a dream

The angel man
w/Serpents competing
for his palms
& fingers
Finally claimed
This benevolent
Soul

Ophelia

Leaves, sodden
in silk

Chlorine
dream
mad stifled
Witness

The diving board, the plunge
The pool

You were a fighter
a damask musky muse

You were the bleached
Sun
for TV afternoon

horned-toads
maverick of a yellow spot

Look now to where it's got
You

in meat heaven
w/the cannibals
& jews

The gardener
Found
The body, rampant, Floating

Lucky Stiff
What is this green pale stuff
You're made of

Poke holes in the goddess
Skin

Will he Stink
Carried heavenward
Thru the halls
of music

No chance.

Requiem for a heavy

That smile
That porky satyr's
leer
has leaped upward

into the loam[16]

I think the day I finally was forced to realize that no one in the world really knows any more about what's going on than any other person, I kind of lost interest in philosophy as a study of ideas, but philosophy appreciated from the standpoint of how men in the past have used words, have used language. That's why for me poetry is the ultimate art form, because what defines us as human beings is language. The way we talk is the way we think, and the way we think is the way we act, and the way we act is what we are.[17]

The American Night

Long poem as odyssey

as copulation

a grand night long intercourse

between mind & reality

river & flesh

A Cunt-Tree

(how easily the actor
slips into molds (condums)
of speech & Thought.
while passing Thru regions)

American Woman
as

From the American Night Journal

When radio dark night
existed & assumed control
& we rocked in its web
consumed by static
stroked w/fear

we were drawn down
The distance of long cities
riding home thru the open
night alone
launching fever & strange
carnage
from the back seat[18]

   •

Welcome to the American Night
where dogs bite
to find the voice
    the face the fate the fame
To be tamed
    by the Night
in a quiet soft - luxuriant
                car
Hitchhikers line the Great Highway

   •

THE FEAR

Eternal consciousness
in the void
(Makes this ordeal seem almost
                    friendly)

A Kiss in the Storm

(Madman at the wheel
 gun at the neck
 space populous & arching
        cooly)

A barn
a cabin attic

your own face
stationary
in the mirrored window

fear of restroom's
tragic cold
neon

I'm freezing

animal's dead

white wings of
rabbits

grey velvet deer

        •

THE CANYON

The car a craft
in wretched
S P A C E

                 brief gold sparks
              behind a shining car
               The Outlaw Star

Sudden movements

& your past
to warm you
in spiritless
Night

The Lonely HWY
Cold hiker

Afraid of wolves
& his own
Shadow

       •

CHEYENNE

Cheyenne to Denver
  (come in Denver)

Cheyenne you shine
     like a City of Gold

(Is there an inner light?)

Just look in my eyes
You'll be all right

       •

MANTRAS

Fuck Shit Piss Kill
death is riding over the hill
someone's coming to do you ill
Fuck Shit Piss Kill

•

THE CROSSROADS

The Crossroads
      a place where ghosts
      reside to whisper into
      the ear of travellers &
      interest them in their fate

      The Hitchhiker drinks.

    --- I call again on the dark-
      hidden gods of the blood

    --- Why do you call us?
      You know our price.
      It never changes.
      Death of you will give
'   you life & free you
      from vile fate. But
      it is getting late.

    --- If I could see you
      again, & talk w/
      you, & walk a short
      while in your company,
'   & drink the heady brew
      of your conversation. . .

    --- To rescue a soul already
      ruined. To achieve respite.
      To plunder green gold
      on a pirate raid &
      bring it to camp for
      the glory of old.

122

--- As the capesman faces
    poisoned horns & drinks
    red victory. The soldier
    too w/his Trophy --
    a pierced helmet. And
    the ledgewalker shuddering
    his way into inward grace.

--- (laughter) Well then. Would
     you mock yourself?

--- No

--- Soon our voices must
    become as one, or one
       must leave.

    •

FOREST STRONG SANDALS

Forest strong sandals
burnt geometry fingers
around a fire
reading history in blackened
books, charcoal sentence
moot splendid eloquence

Flame-tree
Sire, we met in Eden
the troubled time
we had,
rustling in night leaves
a sniper aimed at our window
a kitten mewing in the blasted
strong air

I must go see

   --- You've found your Voice,
    friend, after all else
    I recognize fast the
    strong sure tones of
    a poet.
    Was it a question of
    search or strangling?
    I wonder
    We never talked
    But welcome, here
    To the campfire
    Share our meal
    & tell us your life
    & the hanging

   --- 1st I screamed
    & I was a child again
    alive, then nothing
    til the age of 5

    Then summers & the racetrack
    I look'd for a girl
    in New Mexican bars
    & found jail
    The prostitute look'd out

her cell & saw
"Fuck God" scratched
on a leprous wall

--- Love to hear you ramble, boy
missionary stallion.
But what of the rest?
The jazzed hiway
in the afternoon

--- I got picked-up
& rode thru the night

--- Did you see any buildings?

--- Did I . . . What was I doing?
We danced a lot.
It made her smile.
I don't remember.

--- The logs are melting
fire's ending.
We must move on.
We'll hear you more
at the next altar

•

MIAMI MORNING

What can I read her,
What can I read her?
on a Sunday morning

What can I do that will
somehow reach her
on a Sunday morning

I'll read her the news of
The Indian Wars
Full of criss-cavalry, blood
& gore
Stories to tame & charm
& more
On a Sunday morning

•

BRIGHT FLAGS

The great hiway of dawn
stretching to slumber
pouring out from her greedy
palms a shore, to wander

Hesitation & doubt
Swiftly ensconced

O Viking, your women
cannot save you
out on the great ship

Time has claimed you
Coming for you

•

THE FORM

The form is a plane above
the earth. A soldier bails
out, leaving his entrails
fluttering, billowing. Scoop'd
down, windy midwife, wrench'd
by the world from her rich
belly, my metal mother,
ripped cord, down & frozen.
Following pilot the eye of
the plane. "Great Eye of Night;"
God on a windscreen,
windscream, wormwind
Trailing.

  (& hide among women
   like a toothless bird)

Burned by air
Burned bad by light
in the

    [gun shot]

126

O Wow
he's shot
& the scarlet news
        (hoarse mute confusion
            of the witness crowd)

Actors must make us think
They're real
Our friends must not
make us think we're acting

They are, though, in slow
Time

My wild words
slip into fusion

& risk losing
The solid ground

So stranger, get
wilder still

Probe the Highlands

•

THE AMERICAN NIGHT

for leather accrues
        the miracle of the streets
the scents & smogs &
        pollens of existence

shiny blackness
        so totally naked, she was
        totally un-hung-up

(Lights now on
  we look around
    to see our fellow
    Travellers)[18]

•

35

VERNON ROYAL LINE

COMPOSITIONS

TAPE NOON

From the Tape Noon Journal

MYSTERY OF THE DREAM

Mystery of the dream
a woman or girl is trying
to appear

The Killer - Mexican, naked
    except for shoes.

People, a family not connected
move at hypnotic cross-lines
out of still frame

2 men, detectives, following
searching, sifting thru
back & side-lit rooms, holding
mute counsel. Hats, suits.
Brothers.

People in a woods, a park.
The Killer lurks in his
    own world.

dreams of children & families
return to the sub-world
to assimilate & guide events

New Orleans, sleep, (death's
friend, death's sister)
cattle, horses,
faces get rubbery, clown-painted,
stupid sly & wise & knowing

The mystery of flight

To be inside the brain of a bird

goal - The end of a goddess
    to slide gracefully &)
Knowledgeably into graveland

The Big dream
        vs.
violent assassination of
    spirit & neck & skull
wounded he arrived

    •

Tunnel where dreams are born

Crossroads
--- dream - cell & star collide

diatomic
night - flight

Stewardess fear plane - death

Marines are grinning, looking
at camera
Seals are screaming their
         strange rifle deaths

Seal – skinning

The eskimos have a delicacy.
Cram sea-gulls, live, beak
feathers & claws, into clay
pots. Seal & let sit, or bury,
until the festive season.
Break shell, slice & eat.
            Sacred meat.

•

"Women" select mate for visual-
physical appeal, then engage
in verbal warfare to test
experience & intelligence quotient.
"My womb needs meat & words."

Pumping air in a tire. Pinball bell
clicks gasoline. Counting.

•

1st wild thrush of fear

When?

--- A phone rings
     There is a knock on the door.
          It's time to go.
               No.

          •

"Have you ever seen God?"
 A symmetrical angel.
Felt? Yes. Fucking. The Sun.
Heard? Music. Voices.
Touched? An animal. Your hand.
Tasted? Rare meat, corn, water
          wine.

          •

car cemetery
the abandoned cars
the color of car paint, new
at night, under neon
the dead reside in cars
--- the old man, dirty
     keeper of the graveyard

children, curious, throw stones

          •

Night. Flood-lit backyard.
Trees & darkness beyond.

Figures, an animal, move
across the yard - stage.

A party is going on
in the house.

A woman raped on her
wedding night.

          •

Old feelings revived by
the rain. Winter city.
Slow wet streets -
languid tires, wipers.

Black couple.

Middle-aged woman
cooing & fluttering
an erotic backbend
from a nylon magazine

Invent a clock on the wall

•

To admit fear creates
a vacuum which must
be filled by action

•

Touch scares because
it ends in sex & does
not an orgy always
end with a victim?

•

Who make us feel foolish
for acting w/our eyes.
Lost in the vanity of the senses
which got us where we are.
Children worship but seldom
act at it. Who needs
temples & couches & T.V.?
We can do it on a sunny
floor w/friends & make
any sound or movement
that comes. Roll on our
backs screaming w/mirth
glad in the guilt of our
madness. Better to be
cool in our worship &
gain the respect of the
ancient & wise weaving
those robes. They know
the secret of mind-change
reality.

                        (playground swings
                          the starved dreams)

What channel are we on?

•

The long sweep of road down
the Canyon Boulevard. The
battered speed-menacing sports
car. Parks. Two angels
leave laughing.

House on the side of a hill.
Conversations in the yard.
The room. Rug. A girl.

"I just want a chance to be
  alive, to live & work"

Youth enters. "Are you going
to make that scene this afternoon?"

"No, I doubt it."

Sensation of being fingered
from behind. Struggling,
being forced. Then lifted to
the swell of a real cosmic dream
Flying, swimming thru space.
Other entities revolving.

A woman or young girl's face
appears, changing, changing
New woman of the future.
Insanely beautiful in her
natural erotic posturing,
Ash blonde. Wise, smiling.
To follow the feel or anticipate
her smile, a danger. A threat
to be met, to flee.

"You are a lover, you are a lover."
Friendly taunting voices.

Old girl-friend enters studio.
Greets each one. I ignore,
eyes closed. A deep female
moan begins to permeate
the air. Unendurable. All
have known her.

What message to me?
A quality of ignorance or
self-deception may be necessary
to the poet's survival.

•

White horse mandala
electric pirate
stations of the cross
Criss-cross
    Cry
    Kree!

•

Money, the beauty of

      (currency
      pale green
        greasy
      ornate
       soft
      furrowed
       texture)

          skin or leather

•

There is an equal pull
inward, a return
to all things.

Muscular imagination.
I have ploughed my seed
thru the heart of the Nation.

•

Enter the slip
of the warm womb tide

Wet labyrinth kiss

digging the wells
& riding the lies

all holes & poles

Walk down a street
A drive to the beach
Drowning man's flash
A town in siege

    •

The Desert
  --- roseate metallic blue
    & insect green

    blank mirrors &
    pools of silver

    a universe in
    one body

    •

    Take-off Orbit Re-entry

    Touchdown

all ball games, finish wires & endings
combine to reach
their mutual conclusion

sweet & cruel, all- swelling
final come

    •

The grand highway
is
crowded
w/
lovers
&
searchers
&
leavers
so
eager
to
please
&
forget.

Wilderness

•

People look strange
on the edge of a stream
The sea is more vast
than your pale mystery
Feel lucky to live here

•

The appliance of theatrical make-up
to an outsider must surely come-off
a grotesque ceremony. My
sister, my brother & her friend.
I needn't have worried. That's
why I am always select in
advertising in local papers.
A few minutes beforehand
to rest the face & dissolve the
hard morose mask of the
preceding day.

•

Leaving the phone-booth,
I was struck by a whiff
of the weird.

Insane old country woman
come to haunt the haunts of town

Hairy legs w/open sores

Florida monster insane
animal baby woman

From what swamp or under-rock
did you crawl to remind
us what we chose to leave?

•

Ghost T.V.
"O God, I'm dead"
Television City
soft sweet iris
animal lens
a rose swallowed
by code of
light

•

Bibulous compound of
muck & mulch milk

Tenebrous connections
in forest & farm

all-swarming dish-like
elegance

Say No More

--- That sure was a mouthful.
--- You said it.

•

humans existing naked
among rocks.
dry bone of quiet revels
an animal among animals
cooking   building   eating

          •

Starfish gluttony
What are the word-forms
      for cosmic encounter
Wedding flesh & mind
    in one body

      The Wedding - dress

young woman lies in bed
festivities below
He steals her - a dream

          •

The needle can't follow
  her rage
Literal hair-raising screams
The Queen of the Magazines

          •

Where'd you learn about
      Satan - out of a book

Love? - out of a box

          •

You must confront
    your life
which is sneaking up
    on you
like a rapt coiled
    serpent

snail-slime

You must confront
                the inevitable
                        eventually
Bloody Bones has got you!

            •

I'm always hungry
war-torn Germany
she saw corpses of soldiers
sailing in the Seine

past faces of drinkers
in sidewalk cafes

•

The record stuck at
    "The instant of your birth"

Forget it!
    Get married. Have babies.

I'm learning to like it
never knowing
leaves a field
free
miner's wives

            •

When you move your
   strange young
      centimeters
         just like that

It will take time
   to get into this safe
      w/your wand

Wild swan

     •

Hope is just a word
   when you think in
         table cloths
Laughter will not end
     her funny feeling
 or assuage our
        strange desire
Children will be born

     •

Cock-pit
I am real
   Take a snapshot of me
He is real, shot
Reality is what has been
     concealed from us
       for so long
birth sex death
we're alive when we laugh
when we can feel the
    rush & spurt of blood

blood is real in its redness
the rainbow is real in
   absence of blood

     •

City of Gold

Platforms, galleries
ministers, snakes
miserable captains
ancient searching
numbers - sinks
stones, stalwart friends
children's clown houses

Waiting
for the sand- storm of
straight junk jewels

•

Sudden attack
stabbed & hacked but no
pain no death

Zone of silence
Sudden powered
      mute strangeness
          & awareness
        most awkward to the mind
          alive w/love & laughter
          & memory sweet of kinder
              times
when we spoke & words
        had soft form by
          a fire

•

Christmas towers
The elephant farts & I
    fall on my arch-type
This is no time for sense
     of humor
Mother's got a tumor
It's only a little rumor
    now
but wait til summer
Almost, but not quite
     enough to put one
       on a bummer
Stuck my thumb in
    pulled out a sewer
Sore loser

      •

Moving into the new house
I construct my Kingdom
out of the 1st dry leaf
of morning, & out of
the odor of the burning log,
& the boat which the young
husband poles solemnly,
his young wife cradling
the infant in her arms
on the floor of the boat
as they cross a weird
channel after the war

      •

A man rakes leaves into
a heap in his yard, a pile
& leans on his rake &
burns them utterly.
The fragrance fills the forest.
Children pause & heed the
smell, which will become
nostalgia in several years.

      •

An appearance of the devil on
a Venice canal. Running,
I saw a Satan or Satyr, moving
beside me, a color'd fleshy
shadow of my secret mind.
Running, knowing, not knowing,
crying.

                    •

A long & greasy look like
the country he claimed
& named 1st
        Americus
land of dream-death
desire
holding sway over many
voyagers

("don't come down here, baby,
    these fools are shooting people")

I could trace the smell
of gun-fire on the phone.
You were my partner.

                    •

Moods, breath, & weathers
in her death were measured
& slow & time-filled
fallen sparrows
sad arrows
our sorrow

Branch out into the
        history of the vine
This is my last time
        round this old vale

                    •

cats on drugs, w/silky
ambient hair
    & eyes

This is the Room
where all things
     lie

They dart like beasts
           in the leaves
The world outside

& people move slyly
     thru dark bright
         towers
An ocean awaits us

Bitter dreams
don't argue w/the moon

breasts beasts floors
& flowers must be
scrubbed clean

For the cunt to lie on

Then we lie upon her
& go rigid
& formless
into linoleum

    •

This is my forest
    a sea of wires.
This gaggle of vision
    is my flame.
These trees are men,
    the engineers.
And a tribe of farmers
    on their Sunday off.

Gods -- the directors.
    Cameras, Greek
Centaurs on the boom,
    sliding w/silent
Mobile grace

Toward me --
    a leaping clown
In the great sun's
    eye.

Grand danger there
    in curved thigh.
The avenging finger --
    lord.

•

Dancing & thrashing
    the reptile summer
They'll be here long
    before we're gone
Sunning themselves
    on the marble porch
Raging w/in against
        the slow heat
Of an invaded town

The Kingdom is ours

•

Awake in a room on tender flesh.
Can I come inside you?
May I come in you?
How did this happen?
I've been so used to other girls.

You came home in that black car.
Yes, black, & met me.
You came home late.

How can this be? I ask.
I remember well & now you say

I threw silver metal dust.

Are these beings? Yes.
How many? Why we don't know.
A strong man should be aware.

•

My hell will be your hell
My earth, your earth
My heaven, yours too

•

The enlightened child struggles
to be born.

•

Beggar fish & suppliant mouse.
Is man wrong to have left the river?

•

"O God," she cried
"I never knew what
it meant to be real.
I thought it was all
a joke, a jewel.
I never let the horror
the sweetness, or dignity
in."

"Let me up to see the window.
Dark riders approach in the sunset,
coming back from raiding parties.
The taverns will be full of laughter,
wine, & later dancing. Later,
dangerous knife throws."

"Antonio will be there & that
whore, Blue Lady, playing
cards w/silver decks &
smiling at the night. And
full glasses held up high &
spilled to the moon."

"I'm sad, so full of sadness."

·

All children mercifully flown
back to the beautiful cave.
The cult of progress.

Mystery of fertility
a god in the dark night
a stranger

A nude lies in a light'd doorway
on a pile of old papers
                & money
a lamp like a lance

·

Poet of the call-girl storm.

She left a note on the bedroom door.
"If I'm out, bring me to."

·

I. POEMS AND WRITINGS

The night of the abortion she
dreamed of a blood-red sea
of embryos, crying to her.

•

Translations of the divine
in all languages. The Blues,
the records get you high,
in armies on swift channels.
The new dreamer will sing
to the mind w/thoughts
unclutched by speech.
Pirate mind stations. Las Vegas T.V.
Midnite showings.

•

They need a lot of music
to atone for their sins
against the great gods
of disorder

•

     Huge hanging testicles
& long thick cock concealed
in the slick grey trousers
of a fish-faced man who
loves to pull fish from
the wet hook. Bleeding,
mute, fish eyes. An
increment of sperm, ever-
flowing, self-generating
fountain of rich jewelled
                warm.

•

The dead will be left
    w/too many buildings

•

The neighborhood children
Thought he was god
The army said he was queer
In prison he turned
jailer. An alcoholic
mystic finder of wells
He spoke 7 languages
& chased his sister & all
out of the house w/a gun
& tried to die

        •

Wild as the lemon
cool as the rain
rest in my sunburst
relax in my secret
            Wilderness

It's the brother, not the past
Who turns sunlight into glass
& threads harps unwithered
                        & unstrung

•

My master just told me
that I'm being sold

        •

In the middle of changing
    dreams
In the midst of doomed
    unconscious days
I chanced to spy "a
    taxi, buddy? you want
    girls, pills, grass?
    I show you good time"

down there
we had a good time
down there

"He can take those kids
& stick 'em up his ass"
"You look bad enough to bite"

One night cabins
Jealous city women

•

Cypress Trees of Monterey
The cool wines of disorder
Looking back - growing slowly older

•

THE FORM IS AN ANGEL

The form is an angel of soul
  from horse to man to boy
   & back again

Music sex & idea are the
  currents of connection

friendship transition

conductor of soul from the
  fat brain of stealth
   to sunset

Work out

Welcome to the night
Welcome to the deep good
  dark American Night

a man gets time to die
  his amber waste

sloven footsteps of swine

in the camps, w/dark black
      lumber
crooked stars have destiny's
      number

Lord help us

•

electric storm
    from the front
barometer at zero
    forest
blue-eyed dog
    strangled by snow
Night storm
    flight-drive thru deserts
neon capitals, Wilderness
    echoed & silenced
      by angels

Angel Flight
    to tobacco farm
the roadhouse
    tomorrow

get ready for the Night
    the rumors on waking
a gradual feeling of
    learning & remembering

imagine a heaven in the
    night-time
      would one member be missing?

•

Leave the informed sense
in our wake
you be Christ
on this package tour
-- Money beats soul --

Last words, last words
out

•

We must tie all these
desperate impressions together[19]

•

If my poetry aims to achieve anything, it's to deliver people from the limited ways in which they see and feel.[20]

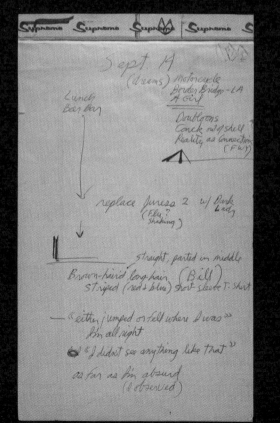

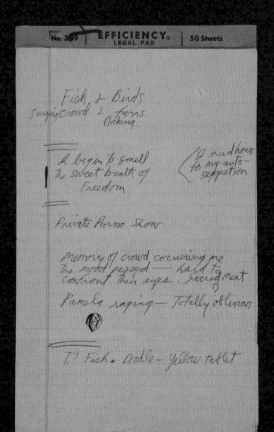

From the Miami Trial Notebooks

Moral decision: To fight
     Defoe

Miami = exercise in self-definition
An ordeal – a time of trial

What are all these woes & poses
Ranting, in the face of an
Infant's deformed hand?

Aug. 12

Drive to Court

Green Entrail, giant metal
esophagus connecting
Court House & Dade County Jail

Rain daylight

Cops holster in escalator mirror
          4 floors
Restroom

Juror's classroom

Ante-room
   to
Church Court
Adrenalin

Press in evidence
Virtual carte - blanche to roam & leer

Channel (Charnal) 4 - Judges lf.

prosecution Judges rt. off - stage folding chair

Stenographer's lips & (Tripod)
    jeweled glasses

    •

desc. Calli & Dща

desc. Hotel

---

attempt to desc. Court corridor
The weird shuffling of eyes

on the Kabuki musicians
desc. relationship thru yrs. a
of band — "The Cats"
maintaining a boyish lightness
of rapport

---

desc. Babe

desc. Tony

Moral decision: To fight
        Defoe

_____

Miami = exercise in self-definition
an ordeal — a time of trial

_____

What are all these woes + poses,
ranting, in the face of an
infants' deformed hand?

_____

1st 6 Jurors

2 Blackmen (green pants, light sport shirt)

woman w/ cane
woman w/ library book

Mr. A
    North in summertime
        N.Y. & Penn.

    asst. veterinarian
    ex - race horse trainer
    Wife & 9 yr. old step twins
    called, never selected for Jury
    Bombardier Navigator Airforce

Mr. B
    (34 yrs) Welder Hialeah
        Widower (voice raises)
          2 daughters 3 grandchildren

    ex- army PFC
    5 times Jury - once criminal case
        One ear

Mr. C
    bachelor, Truck driver Edwards produce
        ex long - distance mover

        arrested on suspicion
        No hard feelings
    Korean War cook

Mrs. D
    Miami Springs 17 yrs
        Husband 1 daughter 2 grandchildren
        Housewife
        Blue dress alive (Poetry?)
    She digs it. Makes rapport (reacts) to other jurors

Mrs. G
  Housewife
   Husband Tax auditor for State
   ex insurance underwrite
    Reading ("all Kinds")
    Book of Mos. Club

John W. Cohn
  young black --- from Georgia
   Transportation at Airidex
   Army - "all in States"
   Wife & 3 kids
--- "Have you ever played in rock or - blues band"
   Shakes head. Mouth open & tongue

  No arrests

  Sustains objection over prejudicial
   Statement of Law

  fingers imaginary moustache

  baseball, no movies or magazines
   his vacation starts Friday

    Would they promise not to hold
    jumping up (objections) against him

  •

Sudden Heat & familiar insidious camera purr
like an insane clock, inevitable & mad

Professional tan & suave of T.V. reporter
Cameraman young & sincere
Tan from living under lights white flare

Suddenly a drab public corridor
becomes a piece of eternity
& on dying leaves us sadder
& shabbier for its brief luster

•

Box Score

18
6X   6X

6

?

•

State has to prove exact charges, no other.

Let me put it another way:
--   defense doesn't have to prove
anything. Pros. has to prove
exact charge, to a moral certainty,
beyond a reasonable doubt

Fundamental law of Land

M. (Max Fink) builds basic dignity of Law

(judge nods occasionally
at Pros. to object)

Abiding conviction in your
mind that lives w/ you.

3000 miles from home
-obj. sympathy & pity.
-He (I) don't want any sympathy
 -He wants Justice.

•

Change tact to Nude Art (classical)

She hasn't seen it.
        She agrees Not guilty, just because used language.
        this is the case, crux

-- You're confusing me so much
right now I don't know what
I'm saying.

-- Do you think sex is dirty? No
        Then apologizes

•

3000 miles from home
- obj. sympathy & pity.
- He I dont want any sympathy
  He wants Justice.

Change tact to Nude Art (Classical
- She hasn't seen it.

she agrees
Not guilty just because used language
This is the case, crux

- You're confusing me so much
  right now I dont know what
  I'm saying.

- Do you think sex is dirty? No
  Then apologizes

Dalpher Edwards

— Rightness is relevant
Right only under Law

(To hear these old phrases forgotten
since school, strange)

— The right way, right passed, that's
what I believe in.
Right is right, wrong is wrong,
Ain't but 2 sides, Just like you
got 2 eyes. The people's change
but right don't ever change,

There ain't but one way, that's the
right way.

M. But under law it's dif.

D. E.

--- rightness is relevant
    Right only under Law

(To hear these old phrases forgotten
    since school, strange)

---   The right way, right passed (past?), that's
    what I believe in.
    Right is right, wrong is wrong.
    Ain't but 2 sides. Just like you
    got 2 eyes. The people's change
    but right don't ever change.

    There ain't but one way, that's the
    right way.

M. But under law it's dif.

    These times are much dif. than
    when you & I were boys.

    When you come to court you don't
    leave your minds at home.

    Is he absolutely innocent in your mind

    •

Lights jade & tickle my vision
green & yellow & opaque Mondrian
window - wood frames
    6 rows of 3

    •

JW "I'm a Hairstylist"

M(arried)?
"No, I'm single"

(Jury dressed better)

Movies, water skiing, night-clubbing
(The Climax)

There are no laws, There are no rules
(confusion here)

Good afternoon Ladies & Gentlemen

> They keep W (tough decision?)

discourse on "Reasonable Doubt"

--- More than one rational
explanation, must decide
in favor of defendant.
--- lack of evidence, also
failure to estab. a fact

[Are Courts Archaic?]
an anachronism

Conference on Media

--- Would everyone take a seat & rise.

Constitutional
Order based on dissent

Was death of Kennedy an obscene act
ob scenus

•

What is this insane staring
& winking by prosecutors

the Brunette as bait; distraction

      Eastman, Ga.   parental copulation
                      unstated inference

      One room farm.   Outhouse
           -- City
      "No, I always never get home"

      - great figures of our history & religion
             had long hair & beards

The Sensuous woman -- he grins
My eyes go to Sec. She smiles
We're all acting for each other
If this is a Quest for Truth. . . .

I turn to look at Gallery
5 rows of Wax figures

"I would hate to injure

Artist as moral catalyst.
It is easier to accept
what exists & adapt
than to try to change it.

    •

one drunken goof
        Men's Room Confrontation
           (signed confession gag)

There once was a group called
           The Doors
Who sang their dissent to the mores,
To be young they protested,
As the witnesses attested,
While their leader was dropping
             his drawers.

? Terry?

Who is the strange criminal
old Rimbaud - like Tanned face
open purple shirt, short
dark hair. furrowed brow
His penetrating eyes.
Can I ask?

"I think he's probably a Leo,

     •

Dinner & Luau
Hurricane & Eclipse

I wish a storm would
come & blow this shit
away. Or a bomb to
burn the Town & scour
the sea. I wish clean
death would come to me.
Feeling of strange Maturity
     hungover
       children of the pool

     •

What is this insane staring
& winking by prosecutors
The Brunette as bait; distraction

Eastman, Ga.   [parental copulation
                [unstated inference
One room farm. Outhouse
        — city
<< No, I always never get home >>

---

                    our
great figures of history & religion
had long hair & beards

The Sensuous woman — he grins,
My eyes go to Sex. She smiles

We're all acting for each other

We excuse Mrs. Truffle

Call
Elaine Hemberly
(No front teeth — effect of hair lip
or freak;
Bum)

"I'm not a selective reader,
I read everything." herson's (23)
+ other

The Exhibitionist

[connect eyes w/ faces, smile or not.
Split decision on possible friend or foe

Count smaller & more human
(natural) than expected.

Hollow silent
No Wigs + Halls

Miami a great deal more
Interesting than my life in LA
Except for dread & squalor
Of Trial appearances
courtroom

       •

Musicians are the cats,
my little gang of cats.
My pets --- dogs, horses, reptiles

       •

The trial is really a trial.

It's an education in human Nature
Funky old human nature.

Your basic human being.
We used to have Barnum &
Bailey's Believe it or not.
Now we have T.V. news.

170   •

chess game/(pure game)

Opening Statements

      Prosecution:
      (1st, argument about films)

      4 knocks on jury door

      presentation of the witnesses

Surprise confrontation
      nervousness of T.(erry)
      initial use of profanity

Our (T.'s) approach- method
- a puzzle to be solved

--- [effort to det.(mine) where to look.
      Jury curious

"The penal area"
"is it your re-election that"

      •

M's performance
      5 min.   30 sec.
      expression of indignant energy

W/in the Realm

      •

Court voyeurs
  people who like childhood
    punishment games

      •

When you hear my words
w/ out good inflection
They sound asinine.

Shouting - Projecting

•

    When the event, The
Night, is over, embers
    cool & ashen, ash-photos,
unclear memories
We are unable to recall
The passion of the evening

    Clinical Courtroom.
      An old photo
      create a myth

Photos
The Artist's sketches
Create beauty out of
This mess of untruths
and poor tapes

like an old photo
requiem for baby pictures

    The Bacchae

(1st day I've sensed
    the possible dignity
    of this drama)

•

AUG 19

beautiful agony of
people being forced, asked,
to remember events in
Time.

  "The word cock or
  something like it"

  Not to impeach, but
    to rehabilitate

  Max's asides for
  jury's ear
          Dionysius plays
          eye-games w/
            the Witness

  •

  AUG 20

---- Mr. Jennings you
    work for the prosecutors
    office, ____
        Signed extradition

  (Scene in hall w/ autographs)

  only way to get
  extradition felony penis

(I have been leading
  commune life, shielded
  from adults.
Sheltered by accountants
            & girlfriends

Miami an education)

    •

Bobby's friend Jim Wood
          ("about up to your shirt pocket")

--- feigning oral masturbation
                uher copulation

        8" -- 12"

-Are you an expert
          on oral copulation

-I don't have a Master's degree

-What studies or investigations
          have you made

-Masturbation
-Circumcision
-Erection

-Stroking (No

Some man up there talking
                Man from Image

                Man w/ young lamb or goat
                Large - brimmed Hat
                Black Cape

Do you consider yourself
          a member of the establishment

No
You deny it.

-What people think of the estab.

-Have you heard "Fuck" in courthouse

Dance in the streets
Stick your toes in the sand
Theatre is where we
          get away w/ murder

This is great
        Max. Get him to deny every
        fucking thing & we'll win!

        Max's out burst
        on his Trial Knowledge
                & ethics

Bobby stumbles twice
        over word
                Supoena (penis

deus ex machina
        evil eye
lights blink

The Kid's lying

Judge smiles as
The Tall one clicks
        out of court

                •

Theatre
"Subtle Shaping of Thought"
old as Aristotle

Children's rhymes
--- English & Nordic
Humpty Dumpty

Plays!

--- no matter how crude,
how rude, even in the street

does not apply to murder
there are only 4 words

"even in Miami Fla.!!"

crude Theatre of Romans
early theatre of the British
Society

Not be embalmed w/ one
set of concepts forever

Plays <u>Most</u> important.

•

3 1/2 yr. cop
undercover (Narc)

bearded
 elegant - hip
  dark
a white male

 500 dope busts
 -did you look in his eyes?
 "glassy & watery"

 a very professional pig

"He was drunk"

 300 times
 Testify for prosecution

•

Writing helps you think

.   .
I think . . I think . .
I speak . . I think
I think . . I feel

        Vague jerky dreams
near morning --
scenes of cowboys & ranch
life -- trading rattle -
snake skins for vials of dope
--- breaking - in of a horse
-- drinks at a bar, someone
from Miami ---- a young
Man burns in a plane &
his antagonist, an older
man, enters inferno to
cradle out charred remains.

I have no servants, only
friends & business associates

        •

Relief of trial (bearable)
& pleasant life here.

To break w/ past (wife
& partners) & define self.

The joy of performing has
ended.

Joy of films is pleasure
        of writing.

        •

Mad airport scramble

Stewards

Short wakes like jet contrails

a Tourquoise sea

rainbow water
&
lightening

Poetry of roulette
& waves

& gran canals

Memories of childhood forests

a small girl
&
a dog

Police released charge
because I was pleasant
& cooperative. Too
tired to be anything else.

difficulty for years
in saying last name.
Send it back in an
        envelope

The appeal of Dionysus was to drive
all ages crazy. The Beatles?
        Not young solely

                    •

Sept. 2

                    Mad airport scramble

                        Stewards

            Short wakes like jet contrails

                    a turquoise sea

                    rainbow water
                         &
                     lightening

                    Poetry of roulette
                        & waves

                    & green canals

            Memories of childhood forests

                    a small girl
                         &
                    a dog

                         •

Sept. 7

The Pirate's Den

--- like all close buddies
we had work'd out an
elaborate system of slang &
imagery to confound our
world of delirium:
Sense of humor, where are you?

•

There's a revolution
        every day -- every time
The sun comes up.

•

discovery of Big People's World
--- after yrs. of protection
        by friends & enthusiasts

Where am I in relation
To Nature & Society.

•

Sept. 13

The advent of R & R
(after its history)
a whiff of water from
The faucet up into the nose
is all I need to call up
those long summer days by the Officer's
Pool.

at the end: I guess
its time to go into
The Desert.

•

Why am I surprised when
    young longhairs make
    intelligent witnesses

The deep Gold Fish Well of Childhood
    cold & green

Call it a day

(They're on their way)

if the jury can beat the rush hour
    let them

       •

Fish & Birds
Surging crowd & fans
       flocking

I begin to smell
The sweet breath of   -
    Freedom

Memory of crowd cornering me
the mood passed --- hard to
confront their eyes. Sacred Meat

       ?
Pamela raging --- Totally oblivious

   •

Judge: Jim M.
doesn't have
a chance.

Judge's chambers (Balloon - Boat & Buffet
      "We may have to separate you two"

            Final Argument

      (Strange aspect of Saturday Court)

            emulation of fellatio
            Coral opulation

He's <u>quisling</u>

Bailiff springy tip-toe

judge looks smaller in suit
his weird smile. dark.

The process of a maturing mind.
Holding on to words.
Nightmare --- slipping back to
            the collective soul.

•

Am I to be one of the Exiles?

Journey thru swamps
& Country

What is my connection
w/ America?

World - Citizen

•

My head is dead

Country road to
cure it

Mts. Streams & Deserts

Vast slow rivers

Crippling cities of Neon

•

Trip after Trial

Thoughts hearken back
& to trips of childhood

1st day	---	Miami	-	Clearwater
2	---	C.	-	New Orleans (2 days)
3	---	N.O.	-	Memphis
4	---	M.	-	Kansas City
5	---	K.C.	-	

•

Subtle but definite changes
in landscape - flat
dense Fla. forest - rolling
into Tall. - tall burnt watery
swamps of LA. - Spanish Moss
-- dif. swamps of Miss.
-- Low dense hills of Alabama
Tin Shacks - rich Farmland of Missouri
drier farms of Iowa

View changed by light -
by time of day

Road Worker - That beer
        Tastes good after hot day

Trucks appear over these corn- hills
like sharks surfacing, like
steel ships - The Sound
        car wafted

going thru short steel bridges

Poetic hierograph of the road
            -- yellow streaks, b & w dashes

Crystallize a trip & memories

        •

Rise & Fall of J. Phoenix

Confess all. Make it
The Tombstone of the Rock
Trip

Miami Blew my confidence
but really I blew it
on purpose

Cheyenne <to Denver
(come in Denver)

Cheyenne you shine
like a City of Gold

(Is there an inner light?)

Just look into my eyes

You'll be all right

Impressionistic Odyssey of
America

w/ HWY as central metaphor

all the beauty horror & vastness

merging personal past
w/ collective present

a child's car ride w/ soft
voices talking

rainbow of headlights

Red tail lights

        •

Why ~~seek~~ the desire for death

A clean paper or a pure
        white wall. One false
line, a scratch, a mistake.
Unerasable. So ~~erase~~ obscure
by adding million other
        Tracings, blend it,
cover ~~it~~ over.

But the original scratch
remains, written in
gold blood, Shining.

Desire for a Perfect Life [21]

•

It was a very interesting trial. I've never seen the judicial system in action; the progress of a trial from the first day to the very last. I had to be there for every day—being the defendant—and it was fascinating; very educational. Maybe I'll write the story of that trial someday. It might be a good journalistic exercise.[22]

COMPOSITIONS

Paris Journal

Paris Journal

So much forgotten already
So much forgotten
So much to forget

Once the idea of purity
born, all was lost
irrevocably

The Black Musician
in a house up the hill

Skeleton in the closet

Sorry. Didn't mean you.

An old man, someone's
                    daughter

Arises

& sees us still in the room
of off-key piano & bad
paintings

him off to work
& new wife arriving

     •

(The candle-forests of
Notre-Dame)

beggar nuns w/moving
smiles, small velvet sacks
& cataleptic eyes

straying to the gaudy
Mosaic calendar
windows

I write like this
to seize you

give me your love, your
tired eyes, sad for
delivery

A small & undiscover'd
park -- we ramble

And the posters scream
safe revolt

& the tired walls barely
fall, graffiti into
dry cement sand

an overfed vacuum
dust-clock

•

I remember freeways

Summer, beside you
Ocean - brother

Storms passing

electric fires in the night

"rain, night, misery --
the back-ends of wagons"

Shake it! Wanda,
fat stranded swamp
woman

We still need you

Shake your roly-poly
Thighs inside that
Southern tent

So what.

It was really wild
she started nude & put
on her clothes.

•

An old & cheap hotel
w/bums in the lobby
genteel bums of satisfied
poverty

Across the street, a
famous pool-hall
where the actors meet

former ace-home of
beat musicians
beat poets & beat
wanderers

in the Zen tradition
from China to the
Subway
    in 4 easy lifetimes

Weeping, he left his pad
on orders from police
& furnishings hauled
away, all records &
mementos, & reporters
calculating tears &
curses for the press:

"I hope the Chinese junkies
         get you"

    •

& they will
for the poppy
rules the world

That handsome gentle
flower

Sweet Billy!

Do you remember
the snake
your lover

tender in the tumbled
brush-weed
sand & cactus

I do.

And I remember
stars in the shotgun
night

eating pussy
til the mind runs
clean

Is it rolling, God

in the Persian Night?

•

"There's a palace
in the canyon
where you & I
were born

Now I'm a lonely man
Let me back into
the Garden

Blue Shadows
of the Canyon
I met you
& now you're gone

& now my dream is gone
Let me back into your Garden

A man searching
for lost Paradise
can seem a fool
to those who never
sought the other world

Where friends do lie & drift
Insanely in
Their own private gardens"

•

The cunt bloomed
& the paper walls
trembled

A monster arrived
in the mirror
to mock the room
& its fool
alone

Give me songs
to sing
& emerald dreams
to dream

& I'll give you love
unfolding

Sun
underwater, it was
immediately strange
& familiar

The black boy's
from the boat, fins & mask,

Nostrils bled liquid
crystal blood
as they rose to surface

Rose & moved strong
in their wet world

•

Below was a Kingdom
Empire of still sand
& yes, party-colored
fishes
-- They are the last
        to leave
        the gay sea

I eat you
avoiding your wordy
bones

& spit out pearls

The little girl gave
little cries of surprise
as the club struck
her sides

I was there
by the fire in the
Phonebooth

I saw them charge
& heard the indian
war-scream

felt the adrenalin
of flight-fear

the exhilaration of terror
sloshed drunk in
the flashy battle blood

•

Naked we come
& bruised we go
nude pastry
for the slow soft worms
below

This is my poem
for you
Great flowing funky flower'd beast

Great perfumed wreck of hell

Great good disease
& summer plague

Great god-damned shit-ass
Mother-fucking freak

You lie, you cheat,
you steal, you kill

you drink the southern
madness swill
of greed

you die utterly & alone

Mud up to your braces
someone new in your
knickers

& who would that be?

•

You know

You know more
than you let on

Much more than you betray

Great slimy angel-whore
you've been good to me

You really have
been swell to me

Tell them you came & saw
& look'd into my eyes
& saw the shadow
of the guard receding
Thoughts in time
& out of season
The Hitchhiker stood
by the side of the road
& levelled his thumb
in the calm calculus
of reason.[23]

•

& sees us still in the room
of off-key piano & bad
paintings

him off to work
+ new wife arriving

  (The candle-forests of
      Notre-Dame) /

beggar nuns w/ moving
smiles, small velvet sacks
+ cataleptic eyes

straying to the gaudy
mosaic/calendar
windows

I write like this
  to seize you

give me your love, your
Tired eyes, sad for
delivery

A small & undiscover'd
park — we ramble

And the posters scream
safe revolt

& the tired walls barely
fall, graffiti into
dry cement sand

an overfed vacuum
dust-clock

& remember freeways

Summer, beside you
Ocean - brother

storms passing

electric fires in the night

'rain, night, misery —
The back-ends of wagons'

Shake it! wanda,
fat stranded swamp
woman

we still need you

Shake your roly-poly
thighs inside that
southern tent

So what.

It was really wild
she started nude & put
on her clothes.

An old & cheap hotel
w/ bums in the lobby
genteel bums of satisfied
poverty

Across the street, a
famous pool-hall
where the actor's meet

former ace-home of
beat musicians
beat poets & beat
wanderers

in the Zen tradition
from China to the
subway
        in 4 easy lifetimes

Weeping, he left his pad

on orders from police
& furnishings hauled
away, all records &
momentos, & reporters
calculating tears &
curses for the press:

‹ I hope the Chinese junkies
                    get you ›

& they will
for the poppy
rules the world

That handsome gentle
flower

Sweet Billy!

Do you remember
the snake
your lover

Tender in The Tumbled
brush-weed
sand & cactus

I do.

And I remember
stars in The shotgun
night

eating pussy
Til the mind runs
clean

Is it rolling, God

in the Persian night?

< There's a palace
in the canyon
where you & I

were born

Now I'm a lonely man
Let me back into
The Garden

Blue shadows
of the Canyon
I met you
& now you're gone

& now my dream is gone
Let me back into your Garden

A man searching
for lost Paradise,
Can seem a fool
To those who never
sought the other world

Where friends do lie & drift
dreamily in

their own private gardens?

The cunt bloomed
& the paper walls
Trembled

A monster arrived
in The mirror
To mock the room
& its fool
alone

Give me songs
To sing
& emerald dreams
To dream

& I'll give you love
unfolding

Sun

underwater, it was
immediately strange
& familiar

the black boy's ~~unthinquietly~~
from the boat, fins & mask,

nostrils bled liquid
crystal blood
as they rose to surface

Rose & moved strong
in their wet world

Below was a kingdom
Empire of still sand
& yes, party-colored
fishes
            — They are the last
                        to leave
the gay sea

I eat you
avoiding your wordy
bones

& spit out pearls

The little girl gave
little cries of surprise
as the club/struck
her sides

I was there
By The fire in the
Phone booth

I saw them charge
& heard the indian
war-scream

felt the adrenalin
of flight—fear

the exhilaration of terror
sloshed drunk in
the flashy battle blood

Naked we come
& bruised we go
just nude pasture
for the slow worms
below

This is my poem
for you   funky & lower'd
Great flowing beast

Great perfumed wreck of h

Great good disease
& summer plague

Great god-damned shyte
mother-fucking freak

you lie, you cheat,
you steal, you kill

you drink the southern
madness swill
of greed

you die utterly & alone
~~in terrible terror~~

mud up to your braces
some~~one~~ new in your
knickers

& who <u>would</u> that be?

you know

you know more
than you let on

much more than you betray

Great slimy angel-whore
you've been good to me

you really have

been swell to me

Tell them you came & saw
& look'd into my eyes
& saw The shadow
of The guard receding
Thoughts in Time
& out of season
The Hitchiker stood
by the side of the road
& I levelled his Thumb
in the calm calculus
of reason.

The King must die
So we can fly
        (I stept into a pile
            of shit)

She died for me!
    (waiter screams down tube,

I didn't mean to kill you
you were just There

COMPOSITION BOOKS

No.	LVS.	RULING
101-30	30	Wide Faint - Margin
101-36	36	Wide Faint - Margin
101-40	40	Wide Faint - Margin
101-48	48	Wide Faint - Margin
101-54	54	Wide Faint - Margin
101-Q-54	54	Quad (5 to the inch)
101-60	60	Wide Faint - Margin
101-P-60	60	Plain - Unruled
101-72	72	Wide Faint - Margin
101-96	96	Wide Faint - Margin
101-108	108	Wide Faint - Margin
104-120	120	Wide Faint - Margin

This Book

No. 101-30

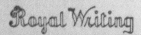

Royal Writing

Notebook and Journal Poems

Mosaic

a series of notes, prose-poems
stories, bits of play & dialog
Aphorisms, epigrams, essays

Poems? Sure[24]

•

December Isles
Hot morning chambers
     of the New Day
Idiot first to awaken (be born)
w/shadows of new play
learned men
in Sunday best
we've had our chance to rest
to mourn the passing of day
to lament the death of our
glorious member
     (she whispers secret messages
       of love in the garden
       to her friends, the bees)
The garden would be here
forevermore

•

The hour of the Wolf
has now ended. Cocks
crow. The world is built
up again, struggling in
darkness.

The child gives in to night -
mare, while the grown man
fears his fear.

I must leave this island,
struggling to be borne
from blackness.

Fear the good deep dark
American Night.
Bless'd is Night.

The flood has subsided
The movie panic & the
chauffeured drive
thru the suburbs.

Wild folks in weird dress
by the side of the hiway

Some of the men wear
tunics or short skirts.

The women posture on
their porches in mock-
classical pose.

The driver aims the car
& it guides itself. Tunnels
click by overhead.

Love the deep green gloom
of American Night.

Love frightened corners,
Thrill to the wood-vine.

So much of it good
& so much quantity.

The Major's boots are where
he left them.

Pseudo-plantation.

Period prints - white
& black boxing match.

A Negro Dance

The principal of the school
holds his nose. "A dead
cow is in there. I wonder
why they haven't sent
someone to remove it?"

A vulture streams by,
& another. The white tip
of his claw-like red beak
looks white, like meat.
Swift sad languorous
shadows.

(Insane couplings out in the night.)

America, I am hook'd to your
cold white neon bosom, & suck
snake-like thru the dawn, I
am drawn back home
your son in exile
in the land of Awakening
What dreams possessed you
to merge in the morning?

"I been in a daze"

A spot, a reef, behind
the nursery door, off
the main bedroom -

The bed looms like a white
funereal butterfly barge
at one end of the room,
hung w/nets & sails.

"We're outlaws."

What church is that?
"Church of God."
white bandana,
white tambourine

Walking on the Water

"In traditional style, we'll
give them a good political
back-siding" - (laughter)

"Victimization"

a frog in the road
children in church
drums

Sun - Sun
lying like death
on the back seat

Revival.

A whore-house.
Lord John & Lady Anne's.
Red-blooded Blue-blooded.
Queen's bosom.

Is it The Princess?

Golden-blood, like me, he said,
folding the bill again neatly,
the Queen's ear - a naked
cock stuck in her ass.

Ha Ha Ha Ha.

You're no more innocent
than a turkey vulture

A cannon

The Negro slaves & the English
killed the Indians, & mixed
w/the Spanish, who were soon
forced out-

Yes, big battles

Boom Boom[25]

•

Airport Virgin
already the French & Negro give
The N.Y. jive
Bar (1st Class Lounge)
The Flight Post Mortem
exchange sig. look w/man
& on plane, w/my rudeness
after being searched & jived
"Are you kidding"
No. dreams
Cognac & queer in Orly
dismal wet streets
Wifely girlfriend jive
desk clerk jive
                (Jive Sunday)
A week of catching time
catching up - Catchup
2 heads on Beaux-Arts Pillars
candy - striped steel arm
The Student Quarter
Drinks in the Aquarium
disorientation & desire for
                        friendship
absence of props
alcohol dreams at dawn

•

When I see a dog

The accumulation of energy

A gathering of forces & symbols

An intersection of ideas
            spheres of interest
            excitement or intense desire

            •

Bitter Winter
Fiction dogs are starving

(The radio is moaning softly
 calling to the dogs
 There are still a few animals
 left in the yard)

Sit up all night
    talking, smoking
count the dead
    & wait 'til morning

Will warm names & faces
    come again?
Does the silver forest end?

            •

What are you doing here?
What do you want?
Is it music?
We can play music.
But you want more.
You want something & someone new.
Am I right?
Of course I am.
I know what you want.
You want ecstasy
Desire & dreams.
Things not exactly what they seem.
I lead you this way, he pulls that way.
I'm not singing to an imaginary girl.
I'm talking to you, my self.
Let's recreate the World.
The palace of conception is burning.
Look. See it burn.
Bask in the warm hot coals.

You're too young to be old
You don't need to be told
You want to see things as they are
You know exactly what I do

Everything

        •

Give me a room w/a polished vieux
Tinted green & a friend I choose
To hold my head, a television
& a bed

Shed a meritorious tear
And have another dream
on me, it's free
you see
you see
you see

        •

I am a guide to the labyrinth
Come & see me
in the green hotel
Rm. 32
I will be there after 9:30 PM

I will show you the girl of the ghetto
I will show you the burning well
I will show you strange people
        haunted, beast-like, on the
        verge of evolution

Fear The Lords who are
secret among us

                •

The Wolf,
who lives under the rock,
has invited me
to drink of his cool
Water.
Not to splash or bathe
But leave the sun
& know the dead desert night
& the cold men
        who play there.

                •

Giant billboards of
the West intrude the beach.
Where once was sidewalk
has become a road

They let us out to see
a movie. Lost in the city.
A bowl of blood, mixed w/
oil, & a small green
Turtle floating upside-down.
        Pieces of garlic.

Incarceration. Slowly,
w/friends patiently around,
velvet beds, irregularly,
in a round room.
Guard tower? In center.

The dining hall.

Impossible to establish
friends on the outside.

A Year & A Day

The Penny Theatre

·

Good-bye Revolution
                Constitution
Good-bye frozen streets
                        on fire
Fancy-dress & Renaissance
            Freaks are leaving for
                        the desert
Soft highways clogged
            w/me escaping
Open fields await us
dirt bikes underneath a
                    new swollen moon

·

One night in Boston, going
back to my room, I was
attacked from behind by
an angry citizen who
thought I had pulled the
fire alarm to wake him.
What he didn't know was
that the electricity was
screwed up thru the whole
building.

One thing more: His
wife defended him, &
she was beautiful.

·

DREAM

Corpse tide express
Wilderness round up

Young girls, identical,
w/black hair, swimming
in the current, chased
by a man w/a knife

He's one of them.
He went in to get food.
Drive away!

The Hotel
Move on to the next room.
Everyone crazier than the
                    next
Super-sane

We had been driving
all night.

Trying to escape the eyes
The City of eyes.

We stopped to get
some food.

He came out. He is
now one of them.

Quick. Get away.

The door flew open.
He dropped the package
running to catch us.

Might as well jump
in the swift river

                •

There was preserved
            in her
The fresh miracle
            of
            surprise

            •

Rambling roan, Xander's daughter

She looked first to the mirror

Secondly, behind her

Bloody novels on her bed

"Time of the Prince"

Her lover had just left

            •

The Night is warm &
            thick w/rest
I can't describe the way
            she's dress'd
She'll cater to some strange
            requests
Anything to please her guests

            •

I received an Aztec wall
            of Vision
& dissolved my room in
            sweet derision
Closed my eyes, prepared to go
A gentle wind inform'd me so
And bathed my skin in ether glow

            •

I received an Aztec wall
                 of vision
& dissolved my room in
                 sweet derision
Closed my eyes, prepared to go
A gentle wind inform'd me so
And bathed my skin in ether glow

Life guard tower
           on diseased beaches
Barks, barks, preaches,
                    Teaches
All must be destroyed
before we reach the city.

each man is his own guide
but heed the tide, please
heed the tide

& then we hide,
shiver, pray,
love & cry.

Now back at the beach
At the top of the sun
We fall in the sand
& greet everyone

Where have we been
They all want to know
And so we tell them :

It isn't high or low
it isn't near or far
its not hard get there
but you can't go by car

NOW YOU MUST LEAVE

Now you must leave
I can't tempt you anymore
Your eyes are liquid
Bandit of tears
Condense all your wisdom
Search in your years
For an image of fever
Coiled in the brain of a snake

Time will tell
Time will tell

Stay a while longer
An eighth of an hour
Part of an arrow
Poised in the fire

Invent new faces
These won't do
The old gets moldy
Withers, dies
Your eyes deceive me
Don't believe me
I could lie

●

Quiet times
it's raining
Curtains gone
& eyes deceiving
Plan your couches
easy, easy
Play your watches mild

Quiet times
Disaster out of doors
Television roars
The woman on the bathroom floor

Turn down your creatures
One by one
& Keep the peace tonite
The mail will reach us
Before noon
We'll mold a new day
Soon.

●

In that year there
was an intense visitation
of energy. I went down to
the beach to live. Sun baked
the days and at night, where
I lay crouch'd on the roof,
the moon became a woman's
face. I discover'd the spirit
of music.

●

Try to excite
A cry in the night
Try to set the Night on Fire (?)

Now you ~~have to~~ must leave
I can't tempt you anymore
your eyes are the liquid
Bandit of tears
Condense all your wisdom
Search in your years
For an image of fever
coiled in the brain of a snake

Time will tell
Time will tell

Stay a while longer
An eighth of an hour
Part of an arrow
poised in the fire ⟶

Invent new faces
These won't do
The old gets moldy
withers, dies
your eyes deceive me
Don't believe me
I could lie

COMPOSITION BOOKS

No. 1148   FAINT RULED
No. 1148-CM COLLEGE-MARGIN
No. 1148¼ QUADRILLE RULED
No. 1148½   UNRULED
No. 1148¾   MARGIN RULED
SIZE 10¾ x 7¾
MADE IN THE U.S.A.

60 LVS.
SECTION SEWED

This Book
No. 1148½

In that year there was an intense visitation of energy. ~~I left school &~~ ~~went down to the beach~~ I left school & went down to the beach. I slept on ~~the~~ a roof, ~~&~~ ~~moon~~ ~~empty ancient~~ abandoned building. ~~At~~ ~~night~~ At night The moon became a woman's face. ~~&~~ I discover'd the spirit of music.

Moment of Freedom
        as the prisoner
        blinks in the sun
        like a mole
        from his hole

        a child's 1st trip
        away from home

        That moment of Freedom

•

The opening of the Trunk

-- Moment of inner freedom
when the mind is opened & the
infinite universe revealed
& the soul is left to wander
dazed & confus'd searching
here & there for teachers & friends.

•

animal scrabbling - back-bending
parliament of dreams - mild
reproach - fair-weather friends
old horse out to pasture - blue
stone tells future - batten
down the hatches - hold me
earnest endeavor to be kind -
their love was a monument -
lend-lease - The lost bird
struck the window - outer-space
is a hand's breath away

•

The dark American Sunset
The night like a vast
        conspiracy to dream, hold
court in the swaying sand
Tijuana - the anus of night
        a cartoon of civilization
Whores are born in the
        American Night

What will we see in the
        bowels of the night, in
The frosted cave where dreams
        are made, right before your
eyes. Prophecy w/out money.

This song must have the sad
common strangeness of currency
coin of the realm. Bitter
embers. Scent of pine smoke
Fire-Night, special breeding
exercises. An excuse for
crime. High School of the
Night. Silence of a school
at night.

•

It has been said that
on birth we are trying
to find a proper womb
for the growth of our
Buddha nature, & that
on dying we find a
womb in the tomb of the
earth. This is my
father's greatest
fear. It shouldn't be.
Instead, he should
be trying to find me
a better tomb.

•

KILROY

Male genitals are small faces
forming Trinities
of Thieves and Christs,
Fathers, Sons, & Ghosts.

A nose hangs over a wall
And two half-eyes, sad eyes,
Mute & handless, multiply
An endless round of victories.

These dry & secret triumphs, fought in stalls,
and stamped in prisons, glorify
our walls, & scorch our vision.

A horror of empty spaces
Propagates this seal on private places.

•

Planes are groaning Mothers
In our feeble insect wars.

Nylon condoms stream behind her Trojan
Warriors on their dreadful writhing flight.

Bailed out, sucked
from her metal belly,
one thin wire is left to prophesy
return,
jump freely.

Swallowing air in the brief canal.
The ground leaps up like dogs
to snap, the field, & rolling pain.

Swamps, rice fields, danger.
Gunned down, over ten of them
struggling w/the wet placenta

While some land back in oceans.
Skin-divers float, free-float,
in the uterus.

The sea is a Vagina which
may be penetrated at any point.

•

On Photography: Photography is a mode of description valued for its incredible accuracy. Its descriptions are false & striking. Light goes about creating its images w/detachment, w/out interference, but like Naturalism in painting, photography has evolved its own system of signs & conventions to assist in the representation.

Photography, now a source for painters, was 1st, in the form of camera obscura, a device for gathering information. Vermeer was 1st to see in it more than a useful tool. On optical projections in darkened rooms he founded a new system of imagery based on the cold & sudden working of light itself. Light strikes & leaves its impersonal record. Vermeer made himself the servant of that light. He purified vision, stripped & refined his art into the semblance of an organic camera.

Discovered by Vermeer:
a new illusion, opposed to naturalism, & the imaginative, strict & unromantic, destroying sentiment completely. Detached in a New Way. At once Images meaningless & infinitely meaningful.
    No longer signs of the physical or spiritual in life, his pictures became truly symbolic; they are the object itself w/out distinction. Metaphor is destroyed. The thing is itself and everything else.

Metaphor as taboo. "Players": the child, the actor, & the gambler. The idea of chance absent from world of child & primitive. The gambler also feels in service of an outside power. Chance is a survival of religion in the modern city, as is theatre, more often cinema, the religion of possession.

238

.

The 'psychic' content of Alchemy, to which chemical researches are a complement, parallel, & useful analogy. Quick-silver or hermetic mercury - symbolic key of creation - comprises the transforming substance that can release energy imprisoned in matter, as well as 'anima', the unconscious desires of the body. It is described as a union of male & female elements. Hermes (mercurius) -- drawn variously as Christ, dragon, or second Adam -- is represented as a unitary being, Hermaphrodite or Androgynous man.

.

Cinema synthesizes the conflict between day & night, sleep & waking, consciousness & uncon., subj. & obj., past & present.

.

<u>Peepshows.</u>   Masturbation stalls.

In peepshows you stand, at the instrument as if urinating, or masturbating in front of a mirror. The cinema requires a more thorough posture of submission. In the peepshow, the Viewer is alone; he assembles his own darkness. The cinema crowd, thru faint signals in the dark, assures itself of a loose alignment against the giant screen phantoms. They spur themselves into possession.

•

First was Comedy, obscene revelry, erotic celebration of the body. All chorus. A dance in a ring of fire. Then cities were born, order, & the idea of a cosmos destroyed the circular concept of time, the erratic, magical control of Nature. Comedy became Tragedy as an audience appeared, & the body was transformed into an image.

•

MASQUE (HAPPENING)

At critical seasons of the year, when the fate of the food supply hangs in balance, mummers appear, dressed in leaves, flowers, beast skins, sometimes masked, blackened or whitened faces, they parade the streets & fields, leaping & shouting, clashing swords, sprinkling water, waving torches, ringing bells, horseplay, indecent jokes & gestures. But in spite of noise & revelry, there is rhythm & purpose in the movements of mummers -- who gather, pass in & out of houses bearing the sacred meat. They drive out into the woods some grotesque person or effigy, the Wild Man. They chase & kill an animal. They choose a sovereign to rule over them. They dance out a Mimic battle in which the grotesque leader is supposed to be slain -- this sham fight sometimes taking the form of a drama in which the hero is married, killed, & brought to life again.

•

The impulse of archaic drama was erotic & sacred. It was all worship, joy, play, celebration. Now we seek safety in theatres, a womb-life that beheads us. We restrict life to the screen at the end of the tunnel. We seek to control life, to impose the gratuitous command which geometry lends us.

•

Goethe's Theory of Vision

The eye arises from light, for light. Indifferent surfaces & organs evolve into their unique form. The fish is shaped by water, the bird by air, the worm by earth. The eye is a creature of fire.

The eye is "light at rest."

But do we create light in the eye?
Is the light our own, or from the world?

>   "Optical illusion is optical truth.
>   It is sacrilege to say that there
>   is such a thing as optical fraud."
>   - Goethe

·

Ancient, universal, ocular superstition: The evil eye, injuring gaze. The look of the fascinator may bewitch, enchant, influence wickedly. To attempt to avoid it is to enhance its power. Injury by vision, impotence, birthmarks miscarriage, any time of significant fertility

·

Man's religious sense arises from his desire to co-create the world. He wants to create, to be god-like. He seeks to assure himself of a magic faculty.

God was originally an Hermaphrodite. He split into 2 opposite beings, & thru their union the world was created.

·

The stages of Magnum Opus depend on the belief that the microcosm of the retort & the microcosm of the universe are one, in all ways identical. On this belief rests the entire Transmutation of metals & permits the adept to compare this chemical evolution w/results in his own being.

The 1st stage is always death, putrefaction of matter, a deliberate return to chaos, to the simplest, innocent perception of the world where man has immediate access to the depths of reality.

In the 2nd stage, these elements are purified. The alchemist gradually senses a seed of new life, an indwelling god, growing w/in him. He becomes suffused w/feelings of joy & oneness w/the world.

The last stage is represented symbolically as a marriage of opposites, wedding flesh & mind, male & female in one body.

•

We must see outside ourselves & reach toward the object instead of sucking it in. We must see w/out the intermediaries, the eyes.

•

Certain drugs, states of drunkenness & exhaustion, lead us toward the unqualified interest in vision, intense & pure, that unfolds the eternal in us.

•

For many the cinema is an emotional wet nurse

Spectators feed on "life" at the breast of the cinema screen.

•

Dreams are at once fruit & outcry against an atrophy of the senses.

Dreaming is no solution

•

Film gives us always the 1st impression, for it has no other.

•

The city is a noble blotch, a cancer.
Orgasm is a compensation for free life where every second is ecstasy.

To regain in a groaning moment what has been sacrificed forever.

·

But the pursuit of vertigo, the impatience of one desiring to be possessed, is no longer the central value in the city - perhaps because ecstasy is 1st of a moral order, & linked desire for chaos & destruction. As a result of displacement in the modern world, it no longer exerts a recognizable attraction, erupting instead in perverse, hypocritical forms, persisting always just below the surface, an underground current of powerful attraction.

·

Man's body is sick. His headlong flight from death leaves no time for joy.

·

Photographs began to replace hand drawn & painted slides. These slide shows immediately preceded cinema in pop favor. Already they employed the complete bag of tricks - close-up, flashback, fades, dissolves - all except movement.

The images they projected were of living models posed before natural or unreal settings. They were usually explorations of serious topics like poverty or white slavery, their stories were never dramatized according. to stage conventions but gave the effect of extreme reality & at the same time, a painting. It was a world of purely visual poetry, minus written text, unconcerned w/details of rational explanation.

Sometimes slides were lost or destroyed.

·

Cinema is best when it is not painting, sculpture, theatre, or language, but an erotic science.

·

My eye is God because It Creates the World.

·

He goes to see the girl
of the ghetto.
Dark savage streets.
A hut, lighted by candle.
She is magician
Female prophet
Sorceress
Dressed in the past.
All arrayed.

The Stars
The Moon
She reads the future
in your hand

•

I am
plainly conscious
of souls forging

•

I want to tell you
about
Texas Radio & The Big Beat

it comes out of the Virginia Swamps
cool & slow
w/plenty of precision
& a back beat narrow
& hard to master
some call it heavenly
in its brilliance
others mean & rueful
of the Western dream

I love the friends I have
gathered together
On this thin raft

we have constructed pyramids
        in honor of our escaping
This is the land where
        The pharaoh died --

Children

The river contains specimens
The voices of singing women
call us on the far shore
& They are saying:
"Forget the Night.
 Live w/us in forests
 of azure,"
(Meagre food for
                souls forgot.)
I tell you this;
    No eternal reward will
Forgive us now for
    Wasting the dawn.

(One morning you awoke
& the strange sun

& opening your door.......)

        •

On the gloom
In the shady living room
Where we lived & died
& laughed & cried
& the pride of our relationship
took hold that summer
What a trip
To hold your hand
& tell the cops
You're not 16
no runaway
The wino left a little in
        the old blue desert bottle

Cattle skulls
        the cliche of rats
who skim the trees
in search of fat

Hip children invade the grounds
& sleep in the wet grass
        'til the dogs rush out
I'm going South!

•

I bring these few rags
        back home this evening
& lay them at your feet
Miserable witness
        to a day of tragic
        sadness & disbelief
Hope you'll find me wanting
Take me to bed
Get me drunk (lay me out)

I dropped by to see you
        late last night
But you were out
        like a light
Your head was on the floor
& rats played pool w/your eyes

Death is a good disguise
for late at night

Wrapping all games in its calm garden

But what happens
when the guests return
& all unmask
& you are asked
to leave
for want of a smile

I'll still take you then
But I'm your friend

        •

Everything human
    is leaving
        her face

Soon she will disappear
    into the calm
      Vegetable
        Morass

Stay!

My Wild Love!

    •

Sirens
Water
Rain & Thunder
Jet from the base
Hot searing insect cry
The frogs & crickets
Doors open & close
The smash of glass
An accidental
Rustle of silk, nylon
Watering the dry grass
Fire -
Bells
Rattlesnakes, whistles, castanets

    •

Sirens
Water
Rain & Thunder
Jet from the base
Hot searing insect cry
The frogs & crickets
Doors open & close
The smash of glass
The soft parade
An accident
Rustle of silk, nylon
Watering the dry grass
Fire
Bells
Rattle snake, whistles, castenets
Lawn mower
Good humor man
Skates & wagons
Bikes

India Ink, Ink of India
There are no more rich colors
Black neon, blocks away
Escapes back smoothly
into desert sea

An appearance of sweat
on Italian silk skin
Slap the rude face
& twist into the doorway

To re-appear, in jewels of glass
as one called the "Gladiator"
Hair claimed by Flame of Fire

Insulting to be back
The dreaded dismal day

Jail is a pussy coil
dry as meat, dog-faced,
clever

We leaped the wall, dog & I
To hang choking on fence collar chain

In this hollow we were born

Mexican Khaki, the green womb
distrust all lovely words like
green & womb

(obey the father, run)
escape back into the landscape
dry as meat, dusty marrow

The car rasps quiet, motor destroys itself
on rotten fuel
The pump is ill, the hose has
a steel nozzle

•

bright pictures of morning

Kee! Kee!

The clouds

Kee!

The Christmas Window

& all-flowing & following falls

O forest follow free

Twice loved, Thrice blest

I love thee

Watch how I love thee

Those were dream days
Stuffed w/stealing
Streaked w/buttermilk eyes
A lot of Trouble, Lover

•

American boy & American girl
Most beautiful people in the world
Son of frontier - Indian swirl
dancing thru the midnight whirlpool
Formless
I hope it can continue
just a little while longer

•

A hole in the clouds
where a mind hides
Pagodas - Temples

in child's raw hope

animal in a tunnel
defined by the light
around him

These evil subsidies
These Shrouds
Surround

•

We awoke, talking. Telling dreams.
an explosion during the night

A new siren. Not cop, Fire,
New York ambulance or European
movie riot news but the strange
siren predicting War. She ran
to the window. The yellow thing
had risen.

•

These children learn to die

                brave electric wheel

The Voice of the Serpent
        dry hiss of age & steam
                & leaves of gold
                    old books in ruined
                        tombs
                The pages break like ash

I will not disturb
I will not go

Come, he says softly

-- an old man appears &
        moves in tired dance
        amid the scattered dead
    gently they stir

            •

Cold electric music
        Damage me
Rend my mind
        w/your dark slumber

Cold temple of steel
        Cold minds alive
            on the strangled shore

Untamed Veterans of psychic Wars

One-night cabins
Jealous city women
Puppets & cruel masters
Cattle
The branding iron
"I want these eyes to weep for me"

pre-war lovers

Anatomy of lace
Mystery of her face

He is safe from the rainbow
He's safe from her smile

He is safe from the window
He's safe from her eyes

The Firehouse

Those moments by a Lake
A street that glows
You know you are here
& certain of the place
your cool face

        •

I know you
I know the child who bore you

Think fast! Is this what you want?
Go behind the bushes. Scalp
you for a nickel, a dime.

Save you in half the time
it takes to remember

This, this is, there is no more:
In spite of all. I still can say

Time is for a'leavin'
Time is for a while
And all we have to grieve us
is more a man a smile
So call your goodbye sister
get her on the line.
& tell all you can miss her
in the gilded marble farm

France is 1st, Nogales round-up   255
Cross over the border --
land of eternal adolescence
quality of despair unmatched
anywhere on the perimeter
Message from the outskirts
calling us home
This is the private space of a
new order. We need saviors
To help us survive the journey.
Now who will come
Now hear this
We have started the crossing
Who knows? it may end badly

The actors are assembled;
immediately they become
enchanted
I for one, am in ecstasy
enthralled
Can I convince you to smile?

No wise men now.
Each on his own
grab your daughter & run

Momentarily. Oxygen
If we need more
Send back for more

Good-night kiss. Strange woman leans over.
Touch her under the nightgown, giggling in the dark.

We will be soldiers in uniform
giving orders. Cows graze

There are buffalo & wild boar
on Catalina.

We just made it.

Curfew curfew

The smoking lamp is lighted
in all authorized spaces.

256   The factory bathroom. Girl,
bend over.

Just some amphetamine.

A madman entered w/gun.
She laughed.

Soon to arrive. Get up there.
The crew is safely aboard
& in the lofty ropes we
Swing & climb the crows
nest swaying, strapped
like ice to the mast all night
      (equator ritual)

All aboard that's going ashore
Can't understand what they're
Saying. All of this Babylon.
She has the smooth moody thighs
      of an old-testament whore.

"I already got him"

He is my friend.

Breach of peace.
On his wedding night.
Transient
Shall I?
Cell life.
The Indian.

Now down & the high-sailing
fluttering of smiles on the air
w/its cool night-time disturbance

       •

like the white wet witch
I fall on your form
& feel frozen

Cancer, the water
of leaves invades
the parlor, Sacred
      & Naked
Now is blessed
    the rest
    remembered

       •

The barn is burning
The race-track is over
Farmers rush out w/
buckets of water
Horse-flesh is burning
They're kicking the stalls
(panic in a horses eye
    that can spread & fill
      an entire sky)

The clouds rush by
& tell a story

of the lightning bolt & the mast
on the steeple

           (the radio is moaning softly
             calling to the dogs
               There are still a few animals
                 left in the yard)

but it's getting harder to describe
Sailors to the undernourished

•

Don't start that panic
Love Street parade

No one's afraid of the law

Someone escaped
to the shore

Your image of me
my image of you
    in
one-night scenes
out on the coast

Won't work anymore

Soft parade
Love Street brigade

•

12:01 A.M.

The Studio is a dark church

Out there the air is no more
                    fit to breathe than death
drive thru Louisville
It makes human beings sick

We're some of the few left
        Trying to give form to a dream

Just what was needed

A small old-fashioned hand-mirror
                in a hall of glass

Nothing. The air outside
Burns my eyes
I'll pull them out
& get rid of the burning

            •

The cigarette burned my fingertips
& dropped like a log to the rug below
My eyes took a trip to dig the chick
Crouched like a cat in the next window
My ears assembled music out of swarming streets
But my mind rebelled at the idiot laughter
The grinding, frightful idiots' laughter
Cheering the war of vacuum cleaners

        (sound of women & vacuums screaming)

            •

The abandoned Hotel
flowers dirt on its walls
The labyrinth of bowels
Moves slowly in grim waste
Children play here, wait
& sway here, Tiring to her
Swoon arched summer
And languid by the bow
Sits Esther, made up
like a queen, port in
a storm, striking fire-bells
in her drawers, chalking
The black street w/wild lies

      •

he enters stage:

Blood boots. Killer storm.
Fool's gold. God in a heaven.
Where is she?
Have you seen her?
Has anyone seen this girl?
              Snap shot (projected)
She's my sister.

Ladies & gentlemen:
     please attend carefully to these words & events
     It's your last chance, our last hope.
     In this womb or tomb, we're free of the
          swarming streets.
     The black fever which rages is safely
          out those doors
     My friends & I come from
     Far Arden w/dances, &
          new music
     Everywhere followers accrue
          to our procession.
     Tales of Kings, gods, warriors
          and lovers dangled like
          jewels for your careless pleasure

      •

I'M ME!

Can you dig it.
My meat is real.
My hands - how they move
balanced like lithe demons
My hair - so twined & writhing
The skin of my face - pinch the cheeks
My flaming sword tongue
spraying verbal fire-flys
I'm real.
I'm human
But I'm not an ordinary man
No No No

•

Fear is a porch where winds
      slide thru in the North

A face at the window that
      becomes a leaf

An eagle sensing its disaster
      but soaring gracefully above

A rabbit shining in the night

•

Some men seem to be rooted
into their souls like firm
planted plants; others wisp
merrily from field to field.

In the center stands a woman,
faint quail & misty pale.
From these two firm parameters
mystery flows onward

Tortures & goes
We two are wed

Yet seldom are we wed

•

LAmerica

cold treatment of our empress
LAmerica

the Transient Universe
LAmerica

Instant communion and
        communication
LAmerica

emeralds in glass
LAmerica

searchlights at twi-light
LAmerica

stoned streets in the pale dawn
LAmerica

robed in exile
LAmerica

swift beat of a proud heart
LAmerica

eyes like twenty
LAmerica

swift dream
LAmerica

frozen heart
LAmerica

soldiers doom
LAmerica

clouds & struggles
LAmerica

Nighthawk
LAmerica

doomed from the start
LAmerica

"That's how I met her,
LAmerica

lonely & frozen
LAmerica

& sullen, yes
LAmerica

right from the start"
Then stop.

Go.
The wilderness between.
Go round the march.

•

Tender island night
And a promise of fever
& scars that burst
     at blossom depth
& more green silver

Black horse hooves galloping sun
Mad chariot race burning
Mad fiery chariot race
Mad girl & mad boy
My feathered son flew
     too near to the sun

•

                    Last words
                    Last words
                       out
                 hisssssssssssss

Tell them you came & saw
& look'd into my eyes
& saw the shadow of the guard
receding

Thoughts in time & out of season
the Hitchhiker stood by the side
of the road
and levelled his thumb
in the calm calculus of reason

                 hisssssssssssss

      •

Midnight
Criminal metabolism of guilt forest
Rattlesnakes whistles castanets

Remove me from this hall of mirrors
this filthy glass

Are you her
Do you look like that
How could you be when
no one ever could

      •

Airport
Messenger in the form of a soldier.
Green wool. He stood there,
off the plane.
A new truth, too horrible to bear.
There was no record of it
anywhere in the ancient signs
or symbols.
People looked at each other,
in the mirror their children's
eyes.
Why had it come.
There was no escape from
it anywhere.
A truth too horrible to name.
Only a loose puking moan
could frame its dark interiors.
Only a few could look upon
its face w/calm.
Most of the people fell instantly
under its dull friendly terror.
They looked to the calm ones
but saw only a green
military coat.

•

Is there a moon in your window
Is madness laughing
Can you still run down beach rocks
bed below w/out him?

Your dog is lost in the frozen woods
        or he would run to you
How can he run to you?
        lunging w/blooded sickness
                        on the snow

A kind lady has taken your poor dog in
and feeds him soft milk, kindness, & white lies

How can he run to you?
He's still scratching streets
& searching strangers for your smell
which he remembers very well.

(Kynaston's bride may not appear
But the odor of her flesh is never very far)

& so we must know you

Why does my mind circle around you?
Why do planets wonder what it
    would be like to be you?

All your soft wild promises were words
Birds
endlessly in flight

•

The Arena

Peace on Earth

I love you
Will you die for me?

Eat me

This way

The end

     •

lulling quiet cry of beauty
dead fawn
muscles delight
in strength

O good great screaming Princess!

Ah, we have fun
& we torture ourselves
& make painful faces
in the windows
to amuse ourselves
as we spend time here

     •

Yes, I can remember
dark totem faces
darker than wet coal
painted, striped
w/reds & greens,
yellow & blue
wiser than night
grinning out of the
evil forest

     •

Connections.

-- What is connection?

-- When 2 motions, thought
        to be infinite & mutually
        exclusive, meet in a
        moment.

-- Of time?

-- Yes.

-- Time does not exist.
    There is no time.

-- Time is a straight plantation

        •

If only I --
        could feel
The sound --
        of the sparrows
& feel childhood
        pulling me
                back again

If only I could feel
        me pulling back
                again
& feel embraced
        by reality
                again
I would die
        gladly die

        •

Suppose we were psychic pirates
That lived upon the land
& couldn't fight the system
We'd have to go w/in

& go w/in we would
w/wood & wine to please
& nary a friendly hand to shake
or a friendly face to greet

& so we'd be green Irishmen
& lackeyed gentlemen Jews
alost on the good ship reality
w/wormwood gaul & booze
                              Ugh!

            •

I fucked the dregs of the ruins
                    of an empire
I fucked the dust & the
                    horrible queen
I fucked the chick at the
                    gates of the Maya
I fucked all your women
                    & treated the same
w/respect for your warriors
                    returned from the
                        Kingdom

fucked w/the Negroes
                    in cabs of the drivers
Fucked little infants of North
                    Indo-China
Branded w/Napalm & Screaming
                    in pain

            •

I don't believe in
        murder
Yet I will not be
        a serf
I can't become a
        scape goat
Cause I still don't
        know my worth
I'm confused as any
        woman
Yet I feel like any
        man
Hermaphroditic saviour
        take it as you can

            •

to get a ship war or
        empire going
    you need the sex
        of conquest
impossible in the family
        context

These wives won't allow
what kind of trip is he on

    I must have madmen for my
                            counsels
    Wizards to decree
        dwarfs in my dominion
    Women on their knees

        please
lets keep the whole thing
        w/in a Theatre

            •

do you have
      straight jackets
for the guests
      yes we do

    •

funny,
      I keep expecting a
knock on the door
well, that's what you
get for living around
          people

a knock? would shatter
      my dreams illusions
      deportment & composure
The struggle of a poor poet
      to stay out of the grips
      of novels & gambling
      & journalism

    •

Whether to be a
        great cagey perfumed
                beast
        dying under the
                sweet patronage
                        of Kings
& exist like luxuriant
        flowers beneath the
        emblems of their
                strange empire
or by mere insouciant
                        faith
        slap them, call their cards
spit on fate & cast hell
to flames in usury

by dying, nobly
        we could exist like
innocent trolls
        propagate our revels
& give the finger to the
        gods in our private
                bedrooms

lets rather, maybe,
                perhaps
        get fucking out in
                the open, & by
swelling, jubilantly
magnificently, end them

        •

THE DEFINITIVE ANTHOLOGY OF JIM MORRISON'S WRITINGS

WITH PHOTOGRAPHS AND HANDWRITTEN EXCERPTS FROM HIS 28 PRIVATELY HELD NOTEBOOKS

THE COLLECTED WORKS OF JIM MORRISON
POETRY, JOURNALS, TRANSCRIPTS, AND LYRICS

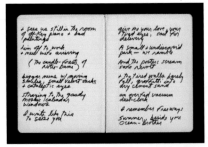

Created in collaboration with the estate of Jim Morrison and inspired by a list entitled "Plan for Book" that was discovered posthumously among his notebooks, this landmark publication and remarkable collector's item includes:

- Published and unpublished work and a vast selection of notebook writings

- The transcript, rare photographs, and production notes of Morrison's final poetry recording

- The Paris notebook, possibly his final journal, reproduced in full

- Excerpts from notebooks kept during his 1970 Miami trial

- The shooting script and color stills from the unreleased film *HWY*

- Complete published and unpublished song lyrics accompanied by numerous drafts in Morrison's hand

- Epilogue "As I Look Back," a compelling autobiography in poem form

- Family photographs as well as images of Morrison during his years as a performer

- Foreword by Tom Robbins; introduction and notes by editor Frank Lisciandro that provide insight to the work; prologue by Anne Morrison Chewning

About the Author

James Douglas Morrison (1943–1971) was a poet, filmmaker, screenwriter, and the lead singer of as well as a lyricist and a composer for The Doors. Prior to his death, Morrison self-published three limited-edition volumes of his poetry: *The Lords/Notes on Vision* (1969), *The New Creatures* (1969), and *An American Prayer* (1970). Simon & Schuster published the combined *The Lords and the New Creatures* in 1970. Posthumous editions of Morrison's writings include *Wilderness: The Lost Writings of Jim Morrison, Volume I* (1988) and *The American Night: The Lost Writings of Jim Morrison, Volume II* (1990).

ISBN 978-0-06-302897-5

9 780063 028975   55000

Available from HarperAudio: The audio book makes available for the first time Morrison's final poetry recording on December 8, 1970, at the Village Recorder, West Los Angeles.

Harper Design
An Imprint of HarperCollins Publishers
www.hc.com

HE FOLLOWS A WOMAN

He follows a woman into the firmament
The solids, sonnets
elaborate requisitions for the god-soul

ah my bright jewelled town
a widow's band
roping sailors & hill-folk together
congeal on this flat spire
to partake of mineral jets
"he's sick" he should be sleeping
peaceful by air, a movie of dead nights
in a wound, suffer to give out
your red-blue lighter's flame
w/calm precision
your certainty lives in a match
or a mind

The huts are free evening cliff-dwellers
The trees, losing their variance, die sadly
w/grandeur
O soft redness & palest blue
              like a baby's window
                This is the hour you rule
          & invite ventures, quests,
          Trips to the electric valley down

There's a whole realm I mustn't tell
traded for a borrowed cell
narrow
The music of poetry & elegant
transformation
makes the whistle on the
visible sun-spell
raise the dog's bark
suffers the children, calling

simply & naturally to their
signalled right doom, the
nude horror & fragment of
a conscious movement
working in time like
a tireless old man
lumbering in the limey landscape
cigarette brilliance, they could
raise mirrors & see them anyway
I've seen horror, we know
each other, lays narcissus
from his cove. The globe is mine.

Uh O. We went to Mexico together
do you remember. Poets pardon
critics who appraise the light
These quarrels are magnanimous
The black cat makes his entrance

Please death be the end

Do not tempt death by naming her
forgive the personal
god-rustle, the couple
in a dog's chain
Let your neighbors know you hear them
to disarm them smile at our failure

confess the weakest image
& fear not the re-write
Seek out the metropolis
Speak out to the North
Testify Providence

alive, w/pulse -
beat of the nation
Miraculous kennel
of Ozark
jamboree

Your face in a face at a friend's
seek better crops
whirl in the
paradise of nymphs & forests

Am I rehearsing for a great
publicast. Can like the president
accept photographs & forgive
time

These days are coming to an end

•

I am troubled
Immeasurably
By your eyes

I am struck
By the feather
of your soft
Reply

The sound of glass
Speaks quick
Disdain

And conceals
What your eyes fight
to explain

•

CLASS PROGRAM

NAME_____ ADDRESS_____

SCHOOL_____CLASS_____

TIME	FROM TO...	PERIOD 1	PERIOD 2	PERIOD 3	PERIOD 4	PERIOD 5	PERIOD 6	PERIOD 7	PERIOD 8
MONDAY	SUBJECT								
	ROOM								
	INSTRUCTOR								
TUESDAY	SUBJECT								
	ROOM								
	INSTRUCTOR								
WEDNESDAY	SUBJECT								
	ROOM								
	INSTRUCTOR								
THURSDAY	SUBJECT								
	ROOM								
	INSTRUCTOR								
FRIDAY	SUBJECT								
	ROOM								
	INSTRUCTOR								
SATURDAY	SUBJECT								
	ROOM								
	INSTRUCTOR								

I am troubled
Immeasurably
By your eyes

I am struck
By the feather
Of your soft
Reply

The sound of glass
Speaks quick
Disdain

And conceals
What your eyes fight
To explain

Woman's Voice:
     The palace of sperm seems warm tonight

Man:
     Umm. gloom gloom doom ruin

Woman:
     Marble porches. The grand ball room.
     Silver smiles. Trumpets. Dancing

Man:
     I want only you

Woman:
     This time come in me like an astronaut
     Send snakes in my orbit

Man:
     We can accomplish miracles
          when we're together

Woman:
     Alone

Man:
     w/the night to guide us

     •

Child tower swirling waters
Cat Monkey pulling force
Chuck Berry getting old
Sit around the floor & play like
       children
Crack-up, like the old days
when kids kept a sense of insanity
going

The crippled folk singer lying
across the road, bundled in
a dirty overcoat, w/his son.
We go to see them out of duty.
He used to share his when he had it
"He had to"

They are both pinioned in wood
w/swollen diseased & bandaged
feet. Eyes closed. No
apparent suffering

They are members of the freak
garden. Flowered eyes.
A lump of flesh all mouth.
A negress, still interested
in fashion w/a fused arm
elbow & thigh.

I swim in a pool w/Negro youths
Mother-fucker.
I climb out. Sorry boys,
Someone's coming. They split.

Residents of the house returning
from the airport. Back entrance.

O Thank you; Thank you
We didn't believe it could still
be so grand, so Magical,

Flowers & light.

The Love Police

On T.V. or Magazine
A Viet Nam encounter,
privately, by young officers
on a beach.

Matador & capes &
sub-machine gun.

•

THE BLUES

O how could this be done to me
great dancer's witness
God, you are a satyr in disguise
Thus cruelly & uselessly to
rend my life awry
I'll lie here stolen, in cold wind
in the road, until peace freezes
                              over,
& hallows me.

280   Rude ghost bastard.

Ah! Who comes now.

•

BOOK OF MEMORY

Albuquerque. W/young men
going up the walk to a party
house. Lights & music. I think
I'll dance tonight. The Shimmy.
Drinking in cars. Stranger
returns for a visit. Low-riders.
Afraid to approach girls.
The company of cars & drinking.

What do the girls wear
What of their hair & eyes
& how do they smell.

•

Clearwater. Mob of cars around
a recreation center in a clearing.
Dance inside. "The Hot Nuts" or
records or local band. Drunk
before arriving. Will she come,
& w/someone else. Making-out
in a car, she came & found me.

   (The sexual sadness of those days
     so hung-up & comic in working
       it out.)

   •

They left me at a Nursery School
while they skied on the slopes.
Tomato soup. I cried, pouted,
& refused to eat. Sort of scolded
when they got back, red-faced
& cheerful.

   •

He threw rocks & cans at the
window, but we didn't awake.
In the same bed? Angry.
Early morning. He had eaten
rattlesnake on flight pattern
to other base.

   •

I am a guide to the labyrinth

Thanks, O Lord, for the
white blind light.
A city rises from the sea.
I had a splitting headache
out of which the future was born.

The Blues

O how could this be done to me
great dancer's witness.
God, you are a satyr in disguise
Thus cruelly & uselessly to
~~make~~ send my life a ~~lie~~ story!
I'll lie here stolen, in cold wind
in the road, until peace freezes
over,
& hallows me.
Rude ghost bastard.
Oh! who comes now.

L.A.

A long way from home, long way
from sight, along the border, tempting
huge reptiles to emerge from slumber,
embattled, we were thrown on the
distance of a long shore. Disparity
reigned. I tell you, no mercury number
could save us now. In the 1st place,
all provisions were wasted

   (In that year we were blessed
   by a great visitation of energy)

and all matter of substance (trade, or barter)
gone. Need prevailed. The wailings of
our distraught messengers. Television
ruled, triumphant. Like a drug that
slowly sickens the mind, she took us.

   The Arrival of the T.V.

Ah, the rule was war, as friendship
faltered. Families quarreled, as usual,
in their chambers. The race suffered.
We travelled. We left home & beauty.
Ah, into these ships, again, we hastened.
The creation of power is slow-wasted.
Borrowed fillings. Brace for the brine.
Heaven kept, hour dated. Winds fermented
Madness & kept parlour rife & rancid.

Crews took leave of sour concubines
& habits. The sea is no place for a lady.
Lads larked & frolicked, pulvering waves
they would seek into the deep. Ark! Ark!

Cathay or Venice. Worlds beyond, &
Worlds after.

This story has no moral.
Trust not sleep or sorrow.
The fife-man croons the lull to wake
& brings strong soldiers to a windy beach

•

Some wild fires
Searchout
a dry quiet kiss on leaving

•

JAIL

The walls screamed poetry disease & sex
an inner whine like a mad machine
The computer
faces of the men

The wall collage
        reading matter

The traders (dealers)

        dropped in a
        cave of roaches
        or rodents

•

789 2284
Alan

L.A.

A long way from home, long way
from sight, along the border, tempting
huge reptiles to emerge from slumber,
embattled, we were thrown on the
distance of a long shore. Disparity
reigned. I Tell you, no mercury number
could save us, Now. In the 1st place,
all provisions were wasted

(In that year we were blessed
by a great visitation of energy)
and all matter of substance (trade, or barter)
gone. Need prevailed. The wailings of
our distraught messengers. Television
ruled, triumphant. Like a drug that
slowly sickens the mind, she took us.

The Arrival of the T.V.

Ah, the rule was war, as friendship
faltered. Familys quarrelled, as usual,
in their chambers. The race suffered.
We travelled. We left home & beauty.
Ah, into these ships, again, we hastened.
The creation of power is slow-wasted.
Borrowed fillings. Brace for the brine.
Heaven kept, hour dated. Winds ferment
Madness & kept parlous rife & rancid.

        Crews took leave of sour conculring
& habits. The sea is no place for a lade
Lads larked & frolicked, pulvering waves
they would seek into the deep. Ark! Ark
Cathay or Venice, Worlds beyond, &
worlds after.

        This story has no moral.
Trust not sleep or sorrow.
The fife-man croons the lull to awake
& brings strong soldiers to a windy bed

monstrously it comes out
lifted out of the wed-lock
& comes out thick & stingy
like to a pain or thin line

          The mushroom
          The unfolding

instant of creation (fertilization)

      not an instant separate from breakfast
      It all flows down & out, flowing

but that instant:

      not fire & fusion (fission) but a moment
      of jellied ice, crystal, vegetative mating
      merging in cool slime splendour.
      a crushing of steel & glass & ice

      (instant in a bar: glasses clash, clink, collide)

far-out splendour

      heat & fire are outward signs of a
      small dry mating

290   •

The end of the dream
will be when it
matters

all things lie
Buddha will forgive me
Buddha will

      •

They send me books
They send telegraphy
Looks like Silly
Symphonys of crime
lost & sudden
T.V. dinner
over the trial, dear
cathartic news

The announcer hums
Hmmmmm. How thoughts
arrive from an
earlier alien time.

Ah, Sweden
a miracle of light
& storms

Wish us Kiss us
goodnite
& bless the borrowed
dawn

A symbiotic relationship

•

Velvet runs the mighty hour
Snow- made touch & hands unite
Here's a union sweet & sour
dangling promises w/light

•

The end of the rainbow

put all my screaming phantasies
into one giant
Box - Trap

image of self-image-propagation
image of elation

Ungulation
limit 1st tree

image of Utopia
a slaughter of phantoms

innocent - guilty

The Human World
bounded by Words
& dust

sweet soft & velvet
dust

292   medium trust

            •

how can we hate or love or judge
        in the sea-swarm world of atoms
        All one, one All
How can we play or not play
How can we put one foot before us
        or revolutionize or write

            •

A ha
Come on, now
luring the Traveller
Mighty Voyager
Curious, into its dark womb
The graves grinning
Indians of night
The eyes of night
Westward luring
into the brothel, into the blood bath
into the Dream
The dark Dream of conquest
& voyage
into night, Westward into Night

       •

Heaven or Hell the circus
of your actions

To Play
(Chance is god here)
at Carnival

assuage the guilt
The deep fear

The separate loneliness

open Sinygog
open Sesame

The party of new connections
Mind made free
Love cannot save you
from your fate

Art cannot soothe
Words cannot tame
The Night

       •

The Moral tight-rope of each waking day

Those who Race toward Death
Those who wait
Those who worry

       •

Men who go out on ships
To escape sin & the mire of cities
Watch the placenta of evening stars
from the deck, on their backs
& cross the equator
& perform rituals to exhume the dead
dangerous initiations
To mark passage to new levels

To feel on the verge of an exorcism
a rite of passage
To wait, or seek manhood
enlightenment in a gun

To kill childhood, innocence
in an instant

       •

night of sin (The Fall)
-- 1st sex, a feeling of having
done this same act in time before
O no, not again

       •

I get my best ideas when the
telephone rings & rings. It's no fun
to feel like a fool - when your
baby's gone. A new ax to my head:
Possession. I create my own sword
of Damascus. I've done nothing w/time.
A little tot prancing the boards playing
w/Revolution. When out there the
world awaits & abounds w/heavy gangs
(of) murderers & real madmen. Hanging
from windows as if to say: I'm bold -
do you love me? Just for tonight.
A One Night Stand. A dog howls & whines
at the glass sliding door (why can't I
be in there?) A cat yowls. A car engine
revs & races against the grain - dry
rasping carbon protest. I put the book
down - & begin my own book.
Love for the fat girl.
When will SHE get here?

•

Does the house burn? So be it.
The World, a film which men devise.
Smoke drifts thru these chambers
Murders occur in a bedroom.
Mummers chant, birds hush & coo.
Will this do?
Take Two.

•

Acid dreams & Spanish Queens
   Lamerica

Asthma child, the fumidor
   Lamerica

Duchess, rabbit, the woods by the road
   Lamerica

Pearl Harbor - Shot off the road
   Lamerica

Conceived in a beach Town
   Lamerica

Relevance of beach or Lakes
   Lamerica

Sinks, snakes, caves w/water
   Florida

   Homo/-sex/-uality
   Lamerica

   Religion & the Family
   Lamerica

Plane crash in the Eastern Woods
   Virginia

Bailing-out over rice-fields
   Lamerica

Guerrilla band inside the town
   Lamerica

Bitter tree of consciousness
   Lamerica

A fast car in the night - the road
   Lamerica

Progress of The Good Disease
   Lamerica

•

4 teen-agers, hand in hand,
a closed circle, eyes closed,
heads bowed by the side
        of the road

Car wreck

later, by the pool
        (we heard the news on
                the radio)

•

The Hitchiker   // Quatrains

The Accident

Angel of Death   epic

The Crossing

The New World (1st night)

Big Dismal

The Christmas Killing

Mosaic

a series of notes, prose-poems
stories, bits of play & dialog
Aphorisms, epigrams, essays
Poems? Sure

L'america

Acid dreams & Spanish Queens
        L'america (another? lone? voice)
Asthma child, The Fumidor
        Lamerica
Duchess, rabbit, The woods by the road
        Lamerica
Pearl Harbor — shot off the road
        Lamerica
Conceived in a beach Town
        Lamerica
Relevance of beach or Lakes
        Lamerica
~~Bismark~~ sinks, snakes, caves' w/ water
        Florida

Homo/sexuality

Lamerica
Religion & the Family
Lamerica
Plane crash in the Eastern Woods
Virginia
Bailing—out ~~over rice~~ rice-fields
Lamerica
Guerrilla band inside the tour
Lamerica
Bitter tree of consciousness
Lamerica
A fast car in the night — The roa
Lamerica
Progress of the Good Disease
Lamerica

Mt. road — to the Picnic
fossils
enlisted men
(drunk, their wives & babies)
sweating in amber
red-faced buddhas
— the sad whistle rocket
no explosion
comes 1st
speed of sound (bomba)

4th of July

---

4 teenagers, hand in hand,
a closed circle, eyes closed,
heads bowed, by the side
of the road

Car wreck
later, by the pool
(we heard the news on
the radio)

Times change, damaged
cat's blood rectify in haste
cactus furrows, wild
thrift catalog of grace

The case bore inward
raise'd wet & westward shadows
to the strange trust
on the south bow

Augment pure shouter's drawl
& light the candle
Night is comin' on
& we're outnumbered

By the waves, each soldier
bristling w/his trowel
To search & claim us
Teach our burial

The mind works wonders
for a spell, the lantern breathes
enlightens, then farewell

Each shipmate oars to understand & eyes unoptic strains
to hear:

We came from over here,
        to over there

Then told we wonder
mindless to degree
Most seldom furls
in slumber, burns
begins a century

•

rich vast & sullen
like a slow monster
come to fat
& die

Madness in a whisper
neon crackle
the hiss of tires
a city growls

a map of the states
the veins of hiways
Beauty of a map
hidden connections

fast trampled forest

Trade-routes
guide lines
The Vikings & explorers
Discoverers
The unconscious

•

Cold White Angel
When his passion mounts
Builds to a nest of feathers
a forest of shoulders & lies
Works melt
        passion spent
        utter one witness
        on the bank, the shore
        listening in tired flattery
        to the new spokesman

•

Put me on your list
        of Victims
        (cock sucked by
          the great city whore)

Kill me
Kill
  Kill
    Kill

America, the great
        syphilitic whore, must
          be purified by fire

I ain't shittin' you Ralph

New Times is comin'

          •

W/the death of print
& population explosion

This will seem no more
Than a sad rant in
the bar of your choice
        signed:
              "death of the poet"

          •

Religion was the
       sperm of the ancient
          parables
They blinded Moses
but we're more modern
So we know where
Fallopian tubes lie
      & the pill is our
             saviour -- the girls
                don't
                 care

No room for
      screwin' in the
      Saintly air

I hear ya

    •

She looked so sad in sleep
Like a friendly hand
just out of reach
A candle stranded on
    a beach
While the sun sinks low
    an H-bomb in reverse

    •

The World consists
of rival gangs
incessantly warring,
roaming the earth,
raping & pillaging
    the planet.

    •

As the slipper gilds
The foot, obscene & golden
& a savage saunters
forth in heat of morning
Leave the self-reliant
boy his loathing

    •

Mexican parachute
blue green pink
invented of silk
& stretched on grass
Draped in the trees
of a Mexican Park
T-shirt boys
in their slumbering
art

•

Soon they will be here
Who?
O gentle listener, soon

I write these words in
the narrow privacy of my cell
to a Mexican girl

Jailer, I hear your keys
dangling & clamoring
in the long hallway

Great Hiway
along the great ocean
I can give you a ride
a little farther up the line

Toward the City

•

The Universe, one line, is a
long snake, & we each are
facets on its jeweled skin.
It moves inexorably, slowly
winding peristaltic intestinal
phallic orgasmic ass-wriggling
slow. Fuck shit piss kill.
The skin of the dead beast
shivers in hair-raising waves
of love. Die brute. Claim
your world. Join the snake
on its slow journey.

The eye of the pilot plane
screams mute cloudily,
the head jet
sensing the city. Streak
to the stars

But old snake mover & god
rolls slow in its progress
around to the end. If he
bites his own tail the earth will
be born.

•

carbine-like treading masher
the Mongols appear on small horses
over a snow-rise

The crisp lamp
holds us
in suspense
Relations on a Sunday
evening

stand fast
          be careful
you can not trust him

you can't on this frozen
moment
you can't on this planet

•

Tell them you came & saw
& looked into my eyes &
watched the shadows of the
guard receding. Thoughts
in Time or out of season
the hitchhiker stood by the
side of the road & levelled
his thumb in the cool,
calm calculus of reason.

    Shhhhhh
      hiss of tires

    •

Hey monkey
wipe your nose
You're poisoned w/books

    All the poets
      trapped, lost, stone-dead
in the dog-shit caverns of
the past (pagodas, temples)

    We, truly, are alive

Man is defined by language
I talk, ? I am
All ideas can be reduced to shit
Not so words & their combinations
The great philosophers are the great
                poets
And the mathematicians
Poetry has a harmony &
majesty which cannot ever
         be denied

    •

Impossible garden
a beautiful savage
like me
poised in a wheat field
ripe w/life
but stranded
peering into the desert
world of old slack
crones by fires
old spectral dudes
w/silver hair,
& doubles, & beast-selves
rangers, silence,
horses

only a new dog
for friendship

& after thumbing gradually
back, the most insane neon
whore in Christendom
languid by
ruins.

•

Now you are in danger
old sheep
Now you are in danger

When the true King's murderers
are allowed to run free
A 1000 Magicians arise
in the night

So I say have fun
& until the whole shithouse
goes up in smoke
grab your favorite girl
& run

Can't you feel it now
that spring has come
It's time to play
in the scattered sun
it's time to run

Let the piper call the tune
March April May June

We're just 2 of a kind
Just 2 of a kind
You want yours & I want mine
Just 2 of a kind

•

Sexy
Deep dark American night
Dark sad endless light

Inaugurated by silence
Winter sadness in the calm cars

Winter photography
Our love's in jeopardy
Sit up all night
Talking smoking
Count the dead, & wait for morning
Will warm names & faces come again
does the silver forest end?

Motel Money Murder Madness
Change the mood from glad to sadness

Corruption of power
Masters working
Holy endless monastic
escapes to caves

•

Tell all the creatures in the street
It's time to eat
Sacred Meat

Tell all the creatures in the street
Will set them free
Sacred Meat

•

Create my face
in the mirror of your
turning world
play it again
& again

Energy passes in the junglish
                              Night
From the bishop to the whore
The president's body guard,
Loves Lulu
Bartender, you collect your dues
& don't forget Macon
Land of the black king
The motel keeper & the maid
who saves your scattered bottles
to raise candles
Immense strings of neon beads
from the host mother, parasite
unnatural lover of dogs

Crucial enemies of respect
Shark-toothed scoundrels
bent on gold parties

•

Maids are bickering in the hall
The day is warm
Last night's perfume
I lie alone in this
cool room

My mind is calm & swirling
like the marble pages of an
old book

I'm a cold clean skeleton
Scarecrow on a hill
in April
Wind eases the arches
of my boney Kingdom
Wind whistles thru my mind
& soul
My life is an open book
or a T.V. confession

    •

Hero = someone who gets away
    w/it.

    •

Artaud -- that brave man's
effort to escape the collective
conscience & drive cannibals
down Main Street. These
heroic madmen, doom'd to
failure & bad teeth

Miami a great deal more
interesting than my life in LA
except for dread & squalor
of trial appearances
courtroom

    •

Those indians, dreams, &
the cosmic spinal bebop in blue.
The cosmic horrors. The cosmic
heebeejeebies. A combo of brain
tissue, blood, shit, sweat
sperm & steel, mixed w/grease
& liquid fire, ovaric calendars
magnified on inner
Television lust - face, mirrors
into nothing, great silence
opens layers of prehistoric
Chinese monsters. The mouths,
the mouths, the cellular MAW.
A young Witch from
N.Y. is laying novice hexes
on my brain-pan, projecting
images of embryo development
on my psychology.

Her terrified wildness
disturbs my generals.
Baby, now I dig your
nightmare visions, & your
sadness & your bitchery

But, yet, thank you for
These spells. It gets my
pen moving.

The screaming maggot
group - grope - called life.

It's time for the desert wild.

Lust capital.

Time for an island, get
drunk, write & sail.

•

By virtue of drugs, intelligence
booze & travel, and all
accruements of life on the
road, I have a deep perception
of the world. But also
amazing blindness, eg. children
This makes men like me but
see me as son - clown - fool.
Don't fly boy. But we love to see you burn.

    •

Men invent the Lord our God
& Father in the War against
Women.

    •

We used to have Barnum &
Bailey's Believe It Or Not.
Now we have T.V. news.

    •

SNAKE FARM

--- Man he came down out a
there like - a hobo
lookin' for a freight train

--- that there's a pilot
      snake, he come 3 days before
      a king snake

Greased lightning
Pure gold
Snake oil
Satan
Uncoil'd
Dirty little boys in the back yard
Blues

    •

Forgetting make-up after
Ed Sullivan
That whole show
—The Kid in New York
(playing

I came all the way
from N.Y. to see a ZOO

Circus

High or Low drama

Listen to the well meaning
spectator

America as Bullring Arena

Those indians, dreams, &
The cosmic spinal bebop in blue.
The cosmic horrors. The cosmic
heebeejeebies. A combo of brain
tissue, blood, shit, sweat
sperm & steel, mixed w/ grease
& liquid fire, ovaric calendars
magnified on inner ~~visions~~
Television lust-face, mirrors
into nothing, great silence,
opens layers of prehistoric
chinese monsters. The mouths,
The mouths, The cellerlar maw.
A young ~~novice~~ witch from
N.Y. is laying novice hexes
on my brain-pan, projecting
images of embryo development
on my psychology.

Her terrified wildness
disturbs my generals.
Baby, now I dig your
nightmare visions & your
sadness & your ~~sad~~ bitchery

But, yet, Thank you for
These spells. It gets my
pen moving.

The screaming maggot
group-grope called ~~society~~ life.

Its time for the desert wild.

Lust capital.

Time for an island, get
drunk, write & sail.

"I saw The Hell of women
back There."

Women are obsolete

'Little wine — dig that girl>

We placate women w/
food & song
w/ sex, marriage, babies

You dig Kids, Jim

Yeah, some of them are nice

I like your wife

Democracy of souls
===

James Dean upstairs
to the crippled girl
Lawyers
Doctors Pilots & death

I hadn't taken a trip
for years when I was
a young punk, outcast
& bored, who needed
to feel waves of power
& depression. Acid had
tried to make a mystic
out of me but I fought
it tooth & nail.
Since then I had relied
mainly on alcohol

•

Now those fires & hells
have subsided & we
are left w/a cold
ejaculatory rape

The Savior Bird has been fed.

"The death & resurrection dude"
The Fabulous James Phoenix

Strange new maturity
Booze could not kill or quench it.

Strange charade of the
guardian angels
Progenitors of love & lust
ode to war & demons

The Roof of Wales
Isle of Wight
A ship brews out there
& wind again speaks

•

An old man labors up incline
walkway on electric cart
      ("They are going to be wanting
        late-modern & contemporary
        stories for the next 10 yrs.
        or so & you're the Man.
        That's why I want you to
        Take over for me - I want
        to retire & relax - I only
        wanted to go part way to
        the top)

his cart falters & he turns
it to head back downhill

     •

Essenes Shamans & Adamites

Mystery Christians
Assassins
Heathens
Alchemists
Stoners

&

Jews

Sexual Renegades
Outlaw Mystics
Devils
Pirates of the Prince

Soothsayers
Evangelists
Holy Rollers
Holy Rock & Rollers

•

The day I left the beach

A hairy Satyr running
behind & a little to the
right.

In the holy solipsism
    of the young

Now I can't walk thru a city
street w/out eyeing each
single pedestrian. I feel
their vibes thru my
skin, the hair on my neck
-- it rises.

        •

At times,
in phantasies, I seem'd
bound up in a giant future wave
a psychic liberation army
that would storm the city walls,
assault the citadels of aged
repression. But if these flightful
moments were rare & speedy,
daily facts came crashing
slimy. Airports, bad loves, &
whispers of paranoiac doubt

        •

Monarch of the protean Towers
on this cool stone porch
above the iron island mist
smog-ridden, brown & dusty
sunk in its own waste
breathing its own breath

        •

324

flayed hares w/white booties
Napoleonic women - parrots
Street sweepers branch-brooms
flush streets at dawn
Pinball & pinball dreams
& the Metro below
& young whores - Arcade
The evil theme of Music Lovers

      •

The people always smile
at others when a whore
enters the cafe. Or on
the street, they give them
wide berth, & even step
aside & stare, w/caps
tipped in the air
so she moves like a ship.

      •

Shrill demented sparrows bark
the sun into being. They rule
dawn's Kingdom. The cars -
a rising chorus - then
workmen's songs & hammers
The children of the schoolyard
a hundred high voices.
Complete the orchestration

      •

Accomplishments:

To make works in the face
                of the voice
To gain form, identity
To rise from the herd-crowd

Public favor
Public fervor

Even the bitter Poet - Madman is
                a clown
Treading the boards

      •

Friends - to travel time
w/- We all share a
predicament a past &
a planet   but friends
support image self definition

Do we exist
Does a man on an island

I piss shit fuck kill
            *

        *   *
            I   am

                •

Scour the mind w/diamond
brushes. Cleanse into Mandalas.
Memory keeps us wicked & warm.
The time temple. Who'll go 1st?
Cloaked figures huddled by walls.
A head moves clocklike slowly.
I'm coming. Wait for me.

•

SQUARE OR PLACE OF LIFE

Odor of cooking meat.
Groups hunkered by fires
A plastic skeleton w/pink
organs. A spiel.

Large crowd around
an old story-teller.
Young boy looks askance
at me. Strangers.

Men holding hands. I
dream it. And the
murderer at the teen-age
shack. Refuses to speak.
I'm the One.

                •

People need connectors
Writers, heroes, stars,
leaders
To give life form.

A child's sand boat facing
   the sun.
Plastic soldiers in the miniature
    dirt war. Forts.
Garage Rocket Ships

Ceremonies, theatre, dances
to reassert tribal needs & memories
a call to worship, uniting
above all, a reversion,
a longing for family & the
safety magic of childhood.

   •

Obj. of Theatre

-- you think your lives are
dull & meaningless. Would
you rather be an Oedipus?

   •

An explosion of birds
Dawn
Sun strokes the walls
An old man leaves the Casino
A young man reading pauses
on the path to the garden

   •

Scour the mind w/ diamond
Brushes. Cleanse into Mandala
Memory keeps us wicked & warm
The Time temple. Who'll go 1st.
Cloaked figures huddled by wall
A head moves clocklike slowly
I'm coming. Wait for me.

Song

Regret for chances missed
For good times past
A Harem? You have one.
Couched in imagery

Square or Place
of Life

Odor of cooking meat.
Groups hunkered by fires.
A plastic skeleton w/ sunk
   organs. A spiel.

Large crowd around
      an old storyteller.
Young boy looks askance
at me. Strangers.

Men holding hands. I
   dream it. And the
murderer at the teen-age
   shack. Refuses to speak.
      Im the one.

The Now, the faint or fall
of feeling feathers. Breathing
holding. The microphone wand partner.
Fall into softness. Awake
w/shame. Arise w/new
found strength.

As a child I felt embraced
by reality. This ended.
To procreate you must
become a self - a cock.
Stand erect. Now you
can slide back into
feeling - tree.

•

THE SIDEWALKERS

The sidewalkers moved faster
We joined the current. Suddenly
the cops. Plastic shields & visors,
wielding long thin truncheons
like wands, in formation,
clearing the street the other way.
To get near or stay away.
Cafes were taking in tables
putting chairs on upside
down, pulling the steel playpen
safety bars. Whistles as
the vans arrive. Moustached
soldiers. We leave the scene.
Eyes of youth, wary, gleaming.
The Church. A pastoral scene
of guitars, drums, flutes,
harps, & lovers. Past
Shakespeare & Co. The restaurants
w/elegant patrons, cross

Street, the small jazz
district (Story Ville) a
miniature New Orleans.
Negroes in African shirts.
A street brass band.
"Fare well to my web footed friends"
Crowd smiles, jogs, & sings.
Move past. San Michel Blvd.
The Statue. The Seine. Bonfires
of cardboard buzz evilly
down the blvd. Fire-tenders.

Smell of smoke. Approach closer
nearer. Suddenly screams
long warhoops & the crowd runs
back. And as we flee,
they attack from behind,
Pressed against cafe tables.
Subway & news Kiosk - A
girl beaten, her cries. Can't
hear blows. Rain. (Man w/bottle)

Join me at the demonstration

We join groups under trees
& rain. Tall public buildings.

Join us at the demonstration.

•

Laughing girl
Crystal wisdom
Satisfy my soul

Smiling girl
Diamond scissors
castrates while she rolls

_____

My Soul Brother Me

The sidewalkers moved faster
we joined the current. Suddenly
the cops, plastic shields & visors,
weilding long thin truncheons
like wands, in formation,
clearing the street the other way.
To get near or stay away,
cafes were taking in tables
putting chairs on upside
down, pulling the steel playpen
safety bars. Whistles as
the vans arrive. Moustached
soldiers. We leave the scene,
Eyes of youth, wary, gleaming.
The church. A pastoral scene
of guitars, drums, flutes
harps, & lovers. Past
Shakespeare & Co. The restaurants
w/ elegant patrons, cross

Street. The small Jazz
district (Storyville) a
miniature New Orleans,
Negroes in African shirts.
A street brass band,
(Fare well to my web footed friends
Crowd smiles, jogs, & sings.
Move past. San Michel Blvd.
The Statue, The Seine. Bonfires
of cardboard buzz evilly
down the blvd. Fire-Tenders,
Smell of smoke. Approach closer
nearer. Suddenly screams
long Warhoops + The crowd runs
back. And as we flee,
They attack from behind.
Pressed against cafe tables.
Subway + news Kiosk. A
girl beaten, her cries. Can't
hear blows. Rain. (Man w/ bottle

Join me at The demonstration

We join groups under Trees
+ rain. Tall public buildings.

Join us at The demonstration

Air Hotel
An ancient liner
sounds of plane organs
a giant hum, whine, scream

attack of young barbarians
white, short hair
rescued by stallion
Night forest, pulled in fun
down rocks by girl, my
head strikes flint sparks.
Moan of arms, "O such
terrible longing"

Wake up. Hour of the Wolf
reflections on death & the universe

New dream. Incredible
scenes of violence. Slaughter
in suburbs. I leap high, a camera
w/girl & other couple
enter premature wet wakening

•

Time works like acid
stained eyes
you see time fly

The face changes as the heart beats
& breathes

We are not constant
We are not arrow in flight
The sum of the angles of change

Her face changed in the car
eyes & skin & hair remain
the same. But a hundred similar
girls succeed each other

•

Up the stairs of a low hotel
he found her
Totally naked, between 2 men
on a bed.
A short hairy criminal
w/raised boot in one hand
Knife in other
Theatrics
A shoebox of snow

•

Barter Bargin' Man
I'll give you our dreams
to let me pass in this world
as one of them.

Barter Bargin' Man
I'll give you my woman
to satisfy your thirst

Barter Bargin' Man
I thought you would
be satisfied but
you still want my health

Barter Bargin' Man
I can't live without dreams
or my woman Please
help yourself to my health.

Signed by you in our
blood, with a
laughing glance at
life and all that it is and is not.

•

up the stairs of a low hotel
he found her
totally naked, between 2 men
on a bed.
A short hairy criminal
w/ raised boot in one hand
knife in other
Theatrics
A shoebox of snow

What the Greek Fisherman
saw!

Why do I drink?
So that I can write poetry.

Sometimes when it's all spun out
and all that is ugly recedes
into a deep sleep
there is an awakening
and all that remains is true
As the body is ravaged
the spirit grows stronger.

Forgive me Father for I know
what I do.
I want to hear the last Poem
of the last Poet.

Sitting here at dawn naked
neath my coat I feel like
some magic Moses on the
subway of time, looking
for a rhyme, or some
sign. Oh well. What else
have we got left.

The Endless quest a vigil
of watchtowers and fortresses
against the sea and time.
Have they won? Perhaps.
They still stand and in
their silent rooms still wander
the souls of the dead,
who keep their watch on the living.
Soon enough we shall join them.
Soon enough we shall walk
the walls of time. We shall
miss nothing
except each other.

•

Isle of Wight

Sweet torture music
herdsmen
she came in me
polishing jade
empty your cup
so we can fill it again
you have to give all
  you have
To know what you own
She's crazy

The fond guild of silence
sea horse of Joy
The tent girl
The Wedding Dress
Camped for the night
voices footsteps on linoleum
They're talking about me

The Medicine Man

I used up most
    of my last stuff
backing on that last stream
I better wait until
I get there
Or I'll have to
   climb the
     eagles tree.
        again
And steal his wings
  (Best thing
    for
    magic)   wings

It's really hot in here, baby
Planes zoom over. Orange
jet. Helicopter.
How did we get to this
foreign shore.
From a study.
Opens onto Spanish
Courtyard.
STudents. The young
hip boy & girl.
Hasheaters, cigarettes.
The soft parade walks by.
Cant look in Jesus' eyes.
This is your guide
for the journey. A moor.

Loose Page Poems

We must have a
  Theatre
To imitate Murder
  grand theft (auto)
   da fe
& propagation
    &
  Murder
<u>& get away w/it</u>
<u>all invited</u>

Where's the bread?
  contact ME
   at
 8512 Santa Monica Blvd.
   659-1667
NO Freaks!

   •

"I am the King"
Yo creo rio
(I believe in the river)

Languages are the remains
  of lost ecstasies
   The Devil
  is the conscious mind
altho the logical extension
  of the ego is god

We need new names,
  symbols & mythologies
  To play w/

   •

LAMERICA

Clothed in sunlight
restless in wanting
dying of fever

Changed shapes of an empire
Starling invaders
Vast promissory notes of joy

Wanton, willful & passive
Married to doubt
Clothed in great warring monuments
of glory

How it has changed you
How slowly estranged you
Solely arranged you

Beg you for mercy

      •

LAMERICA

Androgynous, liquid, happy
Heavy
Facile & vapid
Weighted w/words
Mortgaged soul
Wandering preachers, & Delta tramps

Box-cars of heaven
New Orleans Nile Sunset

      •

ODE

New York Maidens

everyone has their own magic

There is no death

so nothing matters

High Style

Flash & forgive me

high button shoes

clean arrangement

messy breeding

love's triumph

everlasting hope & fulfillment

                •

pencilled heaven
     my regards
         no when to stop

                •

The diamonds shone like broken glass
Upon the midnight street
And all atop the walls were wet
Their white eyes glint & sleek

Then from afar a gnome appeared
An angel flashed on furry feet
The boulevard became a river
While waiting crowds began to quiver

I was in a motel watching
Whiskey in my hand
Her breath was soft, the wind was warm
Someone in a room was born

•

Mouth fills w/taste of copper.
Chinese paper. Foreign money. Old posters.
Gyro on a string, a table.
A coin spins. The faces.

There is an audience to our drama.
Magic shade mask.
Like the hero of a dream, he works for us,
in our behalf.

How close is this to a final cut?

I fall. Sweet blackness.
Strange world that waits & watches.
Ancient dread of non-existence.

If it's no problem, why mention it.
Everything spoken means that,
its opposite, & everything else.
I'm alive. I'm dying.

•

346

Street. Steel thrust sucking space.
Silent willful turbines, motors
raving

City of clouds, pirates of air.

Land of rainbows & scarlet rare
                    islands.

We are here, parables.

Silent climbers.

The breast engine mattered.
Monster in drag, a tin damsel
Shuddered & flew

Cut spent space
Crazed ace
Collect

The cake- walk.

     •

Bourbon is a wicked brew, recalling
courage mile, refined poison
of cockroach & tree bark, leaves
& fly-wings scraped from the
land, a thick film; menstrual
fluids no doubt add their splendour.
        It is the eagle's drink.

     •

Sweet torture music
herdsmen
she came in me
polishing jade
empty your cup
so we can fill it again
You have to give all
you have
to know what you own
She's crazy

It's really hot in here.

Planes zoom over. Orange
jet. Helicopter.

How did we get to this
foreign shore.

From a study.

Opens onto Spanish
Courtyard.

Students. The young
hip boy & girl.
Hasheaters. Cigarettes.

The Soft Parade walks by.
Can't look in Zeus's eyes.

This is your guide
for the journey. A Moor.

•

An angel runs
Thru the sudden light
Thru the room
A ghost precedes us
A shadow follows us
And each time we stop
We fall

•

POWER

I can make the earth stop in
its tracks. I made the
blue cars go away.

I can make my self invisible or small.
I can become gigantic & reach the
farthest things. I can change
the course of nature.
I can place myself anywhere in
space or time.
I can summon the dead.
I can perceive events on other worlds,
in my deepest inner mind,
& in the minds of others.

I can

I am

•

Fence my sacred fire
I want to be simple, black & clean
A dim nothingness
Please
The sea is green
Smoke
like the child's version of a
Christmas dream
w/no
waking.

•

Ride off silver & vast
Hawks swing in their
            vague arch
I lie here, waiting

        Bird of Prey
        Have you seen
        Don't let me die

Mad piano, mad singing
I got here 1st

Sulphurous sea spent
phosphorous warring waves

Look up here, a branch

•

The original temptation was to destroy.
The Cliffs. The Road. The Walls.
Original heroism - to bluff the elements
of fire. To call creatures into the storm.
The original heroism was to fall. To ball.
The all. Natural man.

To participate in the creation.
To screw things up. To bring things
into being.

The Crossroads where the car hides.
Lies. Resides. A meeting-place
of Worlds. Where dreams are made.
Where anything is possible. Demons
lie.

The car is steel & chrome. The wood-pile.
Top of the pile. The heap. The graveyard.
Where metal is reduced to its common
mute element. To be reborn. A tale
of rebirth in the wilderness. To become
chaos & come back.

2 spade chicks, or a King & Queen,
comment from the balcony.

The types of society pass on the boards.
Microcosm in a thimble.

Original steel. The old man.
You must wait for your friends,
elect a King & Queen & march
        to the lake.

Religion of Matter.

Language dies in the mind. The
tongue thickens. Communication
thru music & voices (interior).

There's only so much meat & matter.

Can I have a brother?
If you take a sister.

                    •

The Crossroads intersection meeting pt.
of all worlds, the place (being) by a road
Where new words come, the Spot,
the place, meeting place of minds
aloft, where the great whirling trains
exist, in the human chain

The poetry of abandoned buildings,
The flash of a death-star,
Outlaw Star

Saw a shooting star
under the tent
phantasy - neighbor's father working
in next yard. To Trespass, be caught
slavery

The fight under the tree
The box
The fort & stolen indian rugs
death of a cat, the burial

discovery of death, crossroads
of New Mexico highway

(The car jacked-up, alone, build fire)

"Indian, Indian, what did you die for"

The golden windows
        (Christian Science parlor)

The men-folk, they can sing
& play the blues
in midnite cabins
get it on

fear black, smile at death
not your own
old fool
you will soon go

follow the girl thru Southern streets
thru the train yard
Turns to look as she disappears
into Sunday house

She smiles into her daddy's house
Send bro out w/the gun
There's a Stranger in my train yard
breaking down the virgin pines
bending down the long green weeds
walking thru the grass, my hair

                •

Humanity begins
        where
        the
        empire
        ended

                •

feast green beast, spurred on by
sex, seasoned in silence, w/held
from slumber, silent in the deep pale
night beast languid a cool cunt
a forest flower awoken now breathe
utter a word of reproach for fair
swifty flyers agony of night
the dream car the outlaw star
now he sits reclines in a terrible mansion
made more monstrous by the dark stroke
of slumber

The car is a purple foil beast dead in the
night. Neon is its sign his rich home
soft luxuriant car death gave grace
shaken to the soil He stood in a strange
centre by the meeting point of worlds
This crossroads of desert flies the
corpse of sand batteries the ignition
What did happen! He screams at camera
Here she lie bleeding, blue wounds
just to tell us in our floppy hats
it's over. The cops are rubber animals
w/surgeons cold pride, w/out their
glamour. The ambulance attendants
are sudden amateurs, good-natured in
this foreign chore. The cliffs no longer
contain faces. "I know what jail is
like" & "I know about time."

So we played the carnival. Car. Carne.
Feast of meat. Celebration of blood

O lucky ones who enjoy the dumb show

The reptile farm. The snake farm.
Woman & Monkey. The sign. The sign.

Search for the tree. The place. The sink
Big Dismal

Goes in 2 ways. Spirit & Meat. (sex)

You cannot join what can't be joined
You cannot travel 2 roads
     (He road off in all directions)
     Hand Grenade

    •

Run down to the landing
sending new creatures
     on the run-down barge
launch passengers
     to the soft shore

Passage quick & narrow
     But all your friends
Shot from the same
     Valley of death
Will be your blast
     Companions
On the new day

Quick! Come back
     to the shore
We will build a boat
We will find an
     island

    •

please like me
     says the shrew
What can I do?
     I love her.

    •

S -- Do you intend to send
     some riotous sperm
     on a warpath w/in me

N-- Fuckin A Yes

S -- A?

N-- Ass. Your wriggling squirming
     cupcake of an ass

S -- O.K.[26]

    •

POETRY RECORDING TRANSCRIPTS

The Elektra Tapes

In that year
We had an intense visitation
                    of energy.

            Far Arden
        Signals (calling them home)

When radio dark night existed
& assumed control, & we rocked in its web
Consumed by static, & stroked w/fear
We were drawn down long from
deep sleep & awaken'd
at dayfall by worried guardeners
& made to be led thru dew wet
jungle to the swift summit, o'er looking
The sea. . . . . .

A vast radiant beach
& a cool jeweled moon.
Couples, naked race down
by its quiet side
& we laugh,
like soft mad children
smug in the wooly cotton brains of infancy.

The music & voices
are all around us.

Choose, they croon
The ancient ones
The time has come again
Choose now, they croon
beneath the moon
beside an ancient lake.

Enter again the sweet forest
Enter the hot dream, come w/us
Everything is broken up
& dances.

Jim: *And at this point we hear... uh, ah, West Virginia mountain music, you know, uh... violins.*

•

Moonshine night
Mt. Village
Insane in the woods
        in the deep trees

Under the moon
Beneath the stars
They reel & dance

The young folk
Led to the Lake
by a King & Queen

O, I want to be there
I want us to be there
Beside the lake
Beneath the moon
Cool & swollen
dripping its hot
liquor
sssssssss

Frozen moment by a lake
A knife has been stolen
The death of the snake

I know the impossible sea
        when the dogs bark

I am a death bird
        Naughty night bird

        •

BIRD OF PREY

Bird of prey
Bird of prey
Flying high
Flying high
In the summer sky

Bird of prey
Bird of prey
Flying high
Flying high
Gently pass on by

Bird of prey
Bird of prey
Flying high
Flying high
Am I going to die?

Bird of prey
Bird of prey
Flying high
Flying high
Take me on your flight

Indians scattered on dawn's hiway bleeding
Ghosts crowd the young child's fragile egg-shell mind.

•

Under waterfall, Under waterfall
The girls return from summer balls
Let's steal the eye that sees us all

Tell them you came, & saw
     & looked into my eyes
And saw the shadow of the guard
     receding

Thoughts in time & out of séason
The hitchhiker stood by the side
    of the road
& leveled his thumb
in the calm calculus of reason

Jim: *And then a car passes.*

Why does my mind circle around you
Why do planets wonder what it
would be like to be you

All your soft wild promises were words
Birds, endlessly in flight.

Your dog is still lost in the frozen woods
or he would run to you
How can he run to you
Lunging w/blooded sickness on the snow

He's still sniffing gates & searching
strangers for your smell
which he remembers very well

Is there a moon in your window
Is madness laughing
Can you still run down beach
rocks bed below w/out him?

·

Winter Photography
our love's in jeopardy
Winter Photography
our love's in jeopardy

Sit up all night,
talking, smoking
Count the dead
& wait for morning

Will warm names and faces
come again?
Does the silver forest end?

•

Winter Photo?

Is there a moon in your window
Is madness laughing
Can you still run down
beach rocks bed below
w/out him?

Your dog is lost in the frozen
woods or he would run
To you
How can he run to you
lunging w/ blooded sickness
on the snow

He's still searching gates
& sniffing strangers for
your smell, which he
remembers very well

All your soft wild promises
were words, birds
endlessly in flight.

Think of walks & nights
on the beach

Diamond Nights

Winter Photography
Our love's in jeopardy

Sit up all night, Talking, smoking
Count the dead & wait for morning

Will warm names & faces
Come again
Does the silver forest end?

(Cypress trees of Monterey?)

Moonshine night in the Mt. Village
Insane in the deep Trees
The young folk
Led to the Lake
By a King & Queen

Well, I'll tell you a story of whiskey and mystics and men
    da da da
And about the believers and how the whole thing began
    da da da

First there were women and children obeying the moon
    da da da

Then daylight brought wisdom and fever and sickness too soon
    da da da

You can try to remind me instead of the other, you can
    da da da

You can help to insure that we all insecure our command
    da da da

If you don't give a listen, I won't try to tell your new hand
    da da da

This is it can't you see that we all have our ends in the band
    da da da
    da da da
    da da da

And if all of the teachers and preachers of wealth were arraigned
    da da da

We could see quite a future for me in the literal sands
    da da da

And if all of the people could claim to inspect such regret
    da da da

Well we'd have no forgiveness forgetfulness faithful remorse
    da da da

So I tell you
    I tell you
        I tell you

We must send away
    hmm mmm

We must try to find a new answer instead of a way
    da da daaaa

·

ORANGE COUNTY SUITE

Well I used to know someone fair
She had orange ribbons in her hair
She was such a trip
She was hardly there
But I loved her
Just the same.

There was rain in our window
the FM set was ragged
But she could talk, yeah,
We learned to speak

And one year
has gone by

Such a long long road to seek it
All we did was break and freak it
We had all
That lovers ever had
We just blew it
And I'm not sad

Well I'm mad

And I'm bad

And two years
have gone by

Now her world was bright orange
And the fire glowed
And her friend had a baby
And she lived with us
Yeah, we broke through the window
Yeah, we knocked on the door
Her phone would not answer,
Yeah, but she's still home

Now her father has passed over
& her sister is a star
& her mother smokes diamonds
& she sleeps out in the car

Yeah, but she remembers Chicago
The musicians and guitars
& grass by the lake
& people who laugh'd
And made her poor heart ache

Now we live down in the valley
We work out on the farm
We climb up to the mountains
& everything's fine

& I'm still here
& you're still there
& we're still around

•

The American Night

What was that?
I don't know
Sounds like guns. . . .
Thunder

My name is the Holy Shay
I come to town this day
to tell my story to the Judge

Judge, Judge, Judge, Judge
the man is not wanted here.

Come to our house, say the Manderino
and tell us why it is you stray so near
And why you run away fast
                          & come back slow
In the middle of the sun
In the middle of the day
When even an idiot goes indoors

•

Adolph Hitler is still alive
                (boo hiss)
I slept w/her last night
                (yea)
Come out from behind that
false mustache Adolph
I know you're in there.
                (laughter)

You favor life
He sides with death
I straddle the fence
And my balls hurt

                •

Hey, man, you wants girls
pills, grass, come-on
I show you good time
This place has everything
Come-on, I show you

Can we resolve the past
lurking jaws joints of time
the base
to come of age in a dry place
holes and caves

The music was new
black polished chrome
& came over the summer
like liquid night
The D.J.'s took pills to stay awake
& play for 7 days

The General's son had a sister.
They went down to see him.
They went to the studio
& someone knew him.
Someone knew the TV showman

370

He came to our homeroom party
& played records
& when he left,
in the hot noon sun,
& walked to his car,
we saw the Chooks
had written F-U-C-K
on his windshield.
He wiped it off w/a white rag
&, smiling cooly, drove away.

"He's rich. Got a big car."

My friend drove an hour each day
        from the Mts.
The bus gives you a hard-on
        w/books in your lap.

We shot the bird
        at the black M.P.

My gang will get you
Scenes of rape in the arroyo
Seductions in cars, abandoned buildings
Fights at the food stand

The dust, the shoes
Opened shirts & raised collars
Bright sculptured hair
Spades dance best, from the hip.

Someone shot the bird
on the afternoon dance show
They gave out free records
to the best couple.

•

Always a playground instructor
        never a killer,
always a bridesmaid
        on the verge of fame,
            or over,
he maneuvered 2 girls
into his hotel room.
One, a friend,
the other, the young one
        a newer stranger,
vaguely Mexican or Puerto Rican.

Poorboys thighs & buttocks,
scarred by a father's belt,
she's trying to rise.
Story of her boyfriend
& teenage stone
death games.

Handsome cat,
dead in a car

Come here
I love you.
Peace on earth
Will you die for me
Eat me
this way
the end

I'm surprised you could get it up
He whips her lightly,
sardonically w/belt.
"Haven't I been through enough"
            she asks

The dark girl begins to bleed
It's Catholic heaven.
I have an ancient Indian crucifix
around my neck.
My chest is hard & brown.
Lying on stained & wretched sheets
w/a bleeding Virgin
We could plan a murder,
Or start a religion

•

(Street Speaker)
There's a strange belief by the
children of man which states
all will be well.

Search on man, calm savior
veteran of wars incalculable greed.
God-speed & forgive you
morning star, fragrant
meadowperson girl.
"Indian Indian
what did you die for?
Indian says nothing at all."

Jim: *Then we hear all these horns honking in the rhythm - da da dat dat dat -
da da dat dat dat - and sirens. . . . distant. . . . approaching.*

•

She's selling news in the market
Time in the hall
The girls of the factory
Rolling cigars
They haven't invented music yet
so I read to them
from the Book of Days
a horror story from the Gothic Age
a gruesome romance
from the LA
Plague

I have a vision of American
Seen from the air
28,000 ft & going fast

A one-armed man in a Texas
                         parking labyrinth
A burnt tree like a giant primeval bird
                         in an empty lot in Fresno
miles and miles of hotel corridors
& elevators filled w/citizens

Motel Money Murder Madness
Change the mood from glad to sadness
        play the ghost song baby.

Jim: *Then we hear the ghost song.*

•

(Science of Night)

Earth Air Fire Water
Mother Father sons & daughters
Airplane in the starry night
First fright
Forest follow free
I love thee
Watch how I love thee.

•

Discovery
Angels & sailors (rich girls)
Backyard fences, tents
dreams watching each other
narrowly
Soft luxuriant cars
Girls in garages
out to get
liquor & clothes
Half gallons of wine
& six packs of beer
Tender corral. Jumped
Humped. Born to suffer
Made to undress in
        the wilderness

•

"Now listen to this:
I'll tell you about
Texas Radio & the Big Beat
Soft driven slow & mad
like some new language

Reaching your head
w/the cold sudden fury
of a divine messenger
Let me tell you about
    heartache & the loss
      of God
Wandering, wandering
in hopeless night

The negroes in the forest
brightly feathered
let me show you the maiden
w/wrought-iron soul
Out here in the perimeter
There are no stars
Out here we is stoned
    Immaculate"

•

Jim: *Then we hear a whistle like a bosun's pipe and the carnival immediately begins…gradually mixing rain, thunder, bullfight, football, playground, war, penny arcade. Babylon, fading.*

One more thing.

Thank you, O Lord
For the White Blind Light
A city rises from the sea
I had a splitting headache
from which the future's made.[27]

•

The Village Recorder Tapes

In that year
we had a great visitation
of energy.

Back in those days everything
was simpler & more confused.
One summer night, going
to the pier, I ran into
2 young girls. The
blonde was called Freedom,
The dark one, Enterprise.
We talked, & they told
me this story.

     Come

for all the world lies
hushed & fallen
green ships dangle
on the surface of
Ocean, & sky - birds
glide smugly among
     the planes
Gaunt crippled houses
Strangle the cliffs
In the East, in the cities
     a hum of life
starting, now come

    •

        & the cool fluttering rotten wind
in a child's hand-print on
      picture window
& the gun cocked & held
resting on the shoulder,
      western style

& fire in the night waiting,
in a darkened house
for the cruel insane breed
from town to arrive

& come poking thru smoke
in the fuel & ashes for milk
& the evil leer on their faces
      barking w/triumph
Who will not stop them?

The hollow tree, where
    we three slept & dreamed
    in the movement of
    whirling shadows & grass
    Tired rustle of leaves

An old man stirs the dancers
     w/his old dance
   darkening
   swift shadows lean on the
     meat of forests
     to allow breathing

Gently they stir
Gently rise
The dead are new-born
    awakening
w/ravaged limbs
& wet souls
Gently they sigh
    in rapt funeral amazement

Who called these dead to dance?
Was it the young woman
   learning to play the "Ghost
   Song" on her baby grand?
Was it the wilderness children?
Was it the Ghost-God himself,

Stuttering, cheering,
chatting blindly?

    I called you up to
    anoint the earth.
    I called you to announce
    sadness falling like
    burned skin

    I called you to wish
    you well, to glory in
    self like a new monster
    & now I call on you
    to pray:

    •

Of the Great Insane
American Night
We sing
sending our gift
to its vast promise

Pilots are a problem
The rain & hungry sea
greedy for steel

Say a soft American Prayer
A quiet animal sigh
for the strong plane
landing

We rode on opium tires
from the colossal
airport chess game
at dawn, new from glass
in the broken night

landed then in quiet
fog, beside the times
out of this strange river

Then gladly thru
a wasted morning
happy to be alive to
signs of life
a dog,
a school girl
are we in Harlem?

•

LAMENT FOR THE DEATH OF MY COCK

Lament for my cock
Sore & crucified
I seek to know you
acquiring soulful wisdom
you can open walls of
mystery
strip-show

How to acquire death
On the morning
show

T.V. death
which the child
absorbs

death-well
mystery
which makes
me write

Slow train
The death of my cock
gives life

Forgive the poor old people
who gave us entry
Taught us God
& the child's prayer
in the night

Guitar player
Ancient wise satyr
Sing your ode
to my cock
caress its lament
stiffen & guide
us
we frozen

Lost cells
The knowledge of cancer
To speak to the heart
& give the great gift
  words
  power
  trance

This stable friend
& the beasts of his zoo
wild-haired chicks
women
flowery in their summit
monsters of skin
each color connects
to create the boat
which rocks the race

could any hell be more
horrible than now
& real

"I pressed her thigh
& death smiled"

death, old friend
death & my cock
are the world

I can forgive
my injuries
in the name of
  wisdom
  luxury
  romance

Sentence upon sentence
words are healing lament.
For the death of my cock's spirit
has no meaning in the soft fire.

Words got me the wound
& will get me well

II. POETRY RECORDING TRANSCRIPTS

If you believe it.
All join now in lament
for the death of my cock
a tongue of knowledge
in the feathered night

boys get crazy in the head
& suffer
I sacrifice my cock
on the altar
of silence

•

BLESSINGS

accept this ancient
wisdom
which has travelled
far to greet us
from the East
w/the sun

Call out to him
from the mountain
high, from high
towers

as the mind
rebels
& wends its way
to freedom

grant us one more day
& hour
the hero of this dream
who heals & guides us

Forgive me, Blacks
you who unite
as I fear & gently
fall on darkness

•

In that year
we had a great visitation
of energy.

A vast radiant beach
& a cool jeweled moon
Couples naked raced
down
by its quiet side
And we laugh
like soft, mad children smug
in the wooly cotton brains of infancy.

The music & voices
are all around us.

Choose, they croon
the ancient ones
The time has come again.
Choose now, they croon
Beneath the moon
Beside an ancient lake.
Enter again the sweet forest
Enter the hot dream
Come with us.

Everything is broken up
and dances.

•

Do you know the warm progress
           under the stars?
Do you know we exist?
Have you forgotten the keys
           to the Kingdom?
Have you been borne yet
            & are you alive?

Let's reinvent the gods, all the myths
           of the ages
Celebrate symbols from deep elder forests

[Have you forgotten the lessons
              of the ancient war]

We need great golden copulations

The fathers are cackling in trees of the forest
Our mother is dead in the sea

Do you know we are being led to
           slaughters by placid admirals
& that fat slow generals are getting
           obscene on young blood

Do you know we are ruled by T.V.
The moon is a dry blood beast
Guerrilla bands are rolling numbers
           in the next block of green vine
amassing for warfare on innocent herdsmen
           who are just dying

O great creator of being
grant us one more hour to
           perform our art
           & perfect our lives

The moths & atheists are doubly divine
                    & dying
We live, we die
& death not ends it
Journey we more into the
        Nightmare
Cling to life
        our passion'd flower
Cling to cunts & cocks
        of despair
We got our final vision
        by clap
Columbus' groin got
                        filled w/green death

(I touched her thigh
            & death smiled)

We have assembled inside this ancient
                    & insane theatre
To propagate our lust for life
                    & flee the swarming wisdom
                    of the streets
The barns are stormed
The windows kept
& only one of all the rest
To dance & save us
W/the divine mockery
            of words
Music inflames temperament

(When the true King's murderers
  are allowed to roam free
  a 1000 Magicians arise
            in the land)

Where are the feasts
we were promised
Where is the wine
The New Wine
            (dying on the vine)

resident mockery
give us an hour for magic
We of the purple glove
We of the starling flight
      & velvet hour
We of arabic pleasure's breed
We of sundome & the night

Give us a creed
To believe
A night of Lust
Give us trust in
The Night

Give of color
hundred hues
a rich Mandala
for me & you

& for your silky
pillowed house
a head, wisdom
& a bed
Troubled decree
Resident mockery
has claimed thee

We used to believe
in the good old days
We still receive
In little ways

The Things of Kindness
& unsporting brow
Forget & allow

Did you know freedom exists
    in a school book
Did you know madmen are
    running our prison
w/in a jail, w/in a gaol
w/in a white free protestant
    maelstrom

We're perched headlong
    on the edge of boredom
We're reaching for death

on the end of a candle
We're trying for something
    that's already found us

We can invent Kingdoms of our own
grand purple thrones, those chairs of lust
& love we must, in beds of rust

Steel doors lock in prisoner's screams
& muzak, AM, rocks their dreams
No black men's pride to hoist the beams
while mocking angels sift what seems

To be a collage of magazine dust
Scratched on foreheads of walls of trust
This is just jail for those who must
get up in the morning & fight for such

unusable standards
while weeping maidens
show-off penury & pout
ravings for a mad
staff

Wow, I'm sick of doubt
Live in the light of certain
South
Cruel bindings
The servants have the power
dog-men & their mean women
pulling poor blankets over
our sailors

      (& where were you in our lean hour)

Milking your moustache?
or grinding a flower?
I'm sick of dour faces
Staring at me from the T.V.
Tower. I want roses in
my garden bower; dig?
Royal babies, rubies
must now replace aborted
Strangers in the mud
These mutants, blood-meal
for the plant that's plowed

They are waiting to take us into
        the severed garden
Do you know how pale & wanton thrillful
        comes death on a strange hour
        unannounced, unplanned for
like a scaring over-friendly guest you've
        brought to bed

Death makes angels of us all
        & gives us wings
where we had shoulders
        smooth as raven's
                claws

No more money, no more fancy dress
This other Kingdom seems by far the best
until its other jaw reveals incest
& loose obedience to a vegetable law

I will not go
Prefer a Feast of Friends
To the Giant family

II

Great screaming Christ
Upsy-daisy
Lazy Mary will you get up
upon a Sunday morning

"The movie will begin in 5 moments"
The mindless Voice announced
"All those unseated, will await
The next show"

We filed slowly, languidly
into the hall. The auditorium
was vast, & silent.
As we seated & were darkened
The Voice continued:

"The program for this evening
is not new. You have seen
This entertainment thru & thru.
You've seen your birth, your
life & death; you might recall
all of the rest - (did you
have a good world when you
died?) - enough to base
a movie on?"

An iron chuckle rapped our
minds like a fist.
I'm getting out of here
Where're you going?
To the other side of morning
Please don't chase the clouds
pagodas, temples

Her cunt gripped him
like a warm friendly
hand.
"It's all right.
All your friends are here."

When can I meet them?
"After you've eaten"
I'm not hungry
"O, we meant beaten"

Silver stream, silvery scream, oooo
impossible concentration

Here come the comedians
look at them smile
Watch them dance
an indian mile
Look at them gesture
How aplomb
So to gesture everyone

Words dissemble
Words be quick
Words resemble walking sticks

Plant them
They will grow
Watch them waver so

I'll always be
a word-man
Better than a birdman

But I'll charge
Won't get away
w/out lodging a dollar

Shall I say it again
aloud, you get the point
No food w/out fuel's gain

I'll be, the irish loud
unleashed my beak
at peak of powers

O girl, unleash
your worried comb

O worried mind

Sin in the fallen
Backwoods by the blind

She smells debt
on my new collar

Arrogant prose
Tied in a network of fast quest
Hence the obsession

Its quick to admit
Fast borrowed rhythm
Woman came between them

Women of the world unite
Make the world safe
For a scandalous life

Hee Heee
Cut your throat
Life is a joke
Your wife's in a moat
The same boat
Here comes the goat

Blood Blood Blood Blood
They're making a joke
of our universe

III

Matchbox
Are you more real than me
I'll burn you, & set you free
Wept bitter tears
Excessive courtesy
I won't forget

IV

A hot sick lava flowed up,
Rustling & bubbling. The idiot took
his mind off his flowers, calling
robins doee. Neat marshall
of enterprise. Thought fall diamond.
You wouldn't know class - if it fell
on your ass.   Indeed.   Motel
Swimming pool.
Ass high in junk.   The paper face.
Mirror-mask, I love you mirror.
Venetian blinds.   Mediterranean
Trot.   Trout-fishing.   What's for
lunch.
Index
of Pool (comfort chair, rod [aluminum]
peel, tan, orange flavor golf ball)

Hit his head on a Texas green
                "ya wanta fight"
hard gloves, worthy of sinners fight
                clean
a hard win

He had been brainwashed for 4 hrs.
The Lt. puzzled in again
   "ready to talk"
No sir - was all he'd say.
Go back to the gym.
   Very peaceful
   Meditation

Shower (of conVenience)
a military station in the desert
looking out venetian blinds
a plane
a desert flower
movie air base
cool cartoon

The rest of the world (?) Travel proving
is reckless & dangerous
Look at the cartoons
of brothels
Stag films

The ship leaves port
EXPLORATION

V

A mean horse of another thicket
   wishbone of desire
   decry the metal fox

  •

In that year
we had a great visitation
of energy.

A vast radiant beach
& a cool jeweled moon
Couples, naked, raced
down by its quiet side
And we laugh like
soft, mad children
smug in the wooly
cotton brains of infancy.

The music & voices
are all around us.

Choose, they croon
the ancient ones
the time has come again.
Choose now, they croon
beneath the moon
beside an ancient lake.

Enter again the sweet forest
enter the hot dream,
come w/us.
Everything is broken up & dances.

•

Well, I'll tell you a story of whiskey & mystics & men
And about the believers and how the whole thing began
First there were women and children obeying the moon
Then daylight brought wisdom and fever and sickness too soon.

You can try to remind me instead of the other, you can
You can help to insure that we all insecure our command
If you don't give a listen I won't try to tell your new hand
This is it, can't you see that we all have our ends in the band

And if all of the teachers and preachers of wealth were arraigned
We could see quite a future for me in the literal sands
And if all of the people could claim to inspect such regret
Well, we'd have no forgiveness, forgetfulness, faithful remorse

So I tell you, I tell you, I tell you we must send away
We must try to find a new answer instead of a way.

•

My name is the Holy Shay
I come to town this day
to tell my story to the Judge
judge judge judge judge
the man is not wanted here.

Come to our house say the Mandarino
And tell us why it is
you stray so near
And why you run 'way fast
and come back slow
In the middle of the sun
In the middle of the day
when even an idiot goes indoors.

•

The sun sucks snakes
Into its eye
What do the dead do
When they die?

•

Earth Air Fire Water
Mother Father Sons & Daughters
Airplane in the starry night
First fright
Forest follow free
I love thee
Watch how I love thee

      •

Have you forgotten
the lessons
of the ancient war

Keep opening doors
in the party skull.
The tunnel of Love.
Strangle the women,
voices, one by one

      •

"Sing to your Daddy
in the house of suede"

Funeral bells are ringing
cemetery deer are singing

Cypress trees of Monterey
The cool wines of disorder

Calmly, looking back
growing slowly
older

      •

I want the kiss of war
to unnerve the nation
Demand transfer
to another station

      •

The Politics of ecstasy are real
Can't you feel them working
thru you
Turning night into day
Mixing sun w/the sea.

•

& Gentlemen of doubt
shout your warnings
to the women of Crete
who have no need for meat
Sweet sacred meat
Come out! Come out!
& eat

•

Ledger domain
Wilderness pain
cruel swimming ambience
sweet swimming fish hook smile
I love you all the while
even w/the little child
by the hand
& squeeze

You're learning
fast

Keep off the walk
listen to the children talk

•

Where are my women
Hiding Hiding
Where are my women
Hiding out

Come out of your little rooms
Come out here
Come out of your little corners

I've got
     Meat
     Sacred Meat

•

THE CROSSROADS

Meeting you at your parent's gate
We will tell you what to do
What you have to do
to survive

Leave the rotten towns
of your father
Leave the poisoned wells
& bloodstained streets
Enter now the sweet forest

•

When warriors leave
the field the soil
is rich & rice
will grow again
& gold

•

Cobra sun / Fever smile
-No man kill me

"Who is this insane messenger?"

In times like these we need
men around us who can
see clearly & speak the truth.

Out of breath
        Raving witness

Who comes?
Asia

        •

I walked thru the panther's living room
And our summer together ended
                    too soon
Stronger than farther
Strangled by night
Rest in my sunburst
Relax in her secret wilderness
This is the sea of doubt
which threads harps
        unwithered
        & unstrung
It's the brother not the past
who turns sunlight into glass
It's the valley
It's me

Testimony from
a strange witness

        •

The flowering
          of god-like people
in the muted air
          would seem
                    strange
to an intruder
of certain size

but this is all we have left
          to guide us
Now that He is gone

          •

leads me from
          line to line
in time of fever

In the stillness of an insect dream
I seem to hear the women scream
out wonderingly for solace
          from the tense soldier

          •

Now listen to this:
I'll tell you about Texas Radio & the Big Beat
Soft driven slow & mad like some new language
Reaching your head w/the cold sudden fury of a divine messenger

Let me tell you about heartache & the loss of God
Wandering, wandering in hopeless night
The negroes in the forest brightly feathered
Let me show you the maiden w/wrought-iron soul

Out here on the perimeter there are no stars
Out here we is stoned immaculate

          •

Help! Help! Save us!
Save us!
We're dying, fella, do something.
Get us out of this!
Save us!
I'm dying.
What have we done now!
We've done it, fella, we've committed the...

Help!
This is the end of us, fella.
I love you fella.
I love you fella.
I love you cause you're you.

But you've got to help us.
What have we done, fella,
What have we done now?

　　　•

Where are my dreamers
Today & tonight
Where are my dancers
leaping madly
whirling & screaming

Where are my women
quietly dreaming
caught like angels
on the dark porch
of a velvet ranch
dance dance dance dance
　　　　　dance dance dance

　　　•

It was the greatest night of my life
Although I still had not found a wife
I had my friends right there beside me
We were close together (2)

Indians scattered on dawn's highway
bleeding
Ghosts crowd the young childs fragile
egg-shell mind

We scaled the wall
We tripped thru The graveyard
Ancient shapes were all around us
No music But the wet grass
felt fresh beside the fog

Two made love in a silent spot
One chased a rabbit into The dark
A girl got drunk & balled the dead
And I gave empty sermons to my
head

Cemetary cool & quiet
Hate to leave
your sacred lay
Dread the milky coming of the day
I'd love to stay (2)

It was the greatest night of my life
Although I still had not found a wife
I had my friends right there beside me
We were close together

Indians scattered on dawn's highway bleeding
Ghosts crowd the young child's fragile egg shell mind

We scaled the wall
We tripped thru the graveyard
Ancient shapes were all around us
No music but the wet grass
                felt fresh beside the fog

Two made love in a silent spot
one chased a rabbit into the dark
a girl got drunk & balled the dead
& I gave empty sermons to my head

Cemetery cool & quiet
Hate to leave your sacred lay
Dread the milky coming of the day

I'd love to stay
I'd love to stay
I'd love to stay

•

Indian Indian what did you die for
Indian says nothing at all

•

WOMAN IN THE WINDOW

I am the woman in the window
See the children playing
soldier sailor young man on your way
To the summer swimming pool

Can you see me standing
in my window can you hear me
laughing
Mmm - mmm

Come upstairs sir, to your room
& I will play for you

Oh, dreamland
Golden sceneland
Try to sleepland
Take us to dreamland
I am unhappy
Far from my woman
Take me to dreamland
Land of the Banyan
Land of plentiful

Pleasures of pines   and
Potatoes on tables
laden with good things.

Eat at my table
she cried to the vineyards
Calling the workers
home from the meadows

Man you are evil
get away from my garden
Ours is a good place
home of the reindeer

Sell me your pony
Your fast golden pony
I need his strength
& his terrible footsteps

Riding the prairie
just me and my angel
Just try & stop us
we're going to love.

Open your window
Woman of Palestine
Throw down your raiment
& cover us over.

•

Jim: *Okay. Now, let's go get a taco.*

The Village Recorder Tapes, Part II

When radio dark night
existed & assumed control
and we rocked in its web
consumed by static
stroked w/fear

We were drawn down
the distance of long cities
riding home thru the open
night, alone
launching fever & strange
carnage
from the back seat.

·

Awake
Shake dreams from your hair
     My pretty child, my sweet one
Choose the day, & choose the sign
     of your day, the days
     divinity, 1st thing you see.

A burnt tree, like a giant
     primeval bird, a leaf,
dry & bitter, crackling tales
     in its warm ways.
Sidewalk gods will do for you.
     The forest of the neighborhood,
The empty lost museum, &
The mesa, & the Mt.'s pregnant
Monument above the newsstand
     where the children hide
       When school ends

·

In this full-throated
Sex'd cry
we must try again
to speak of the ununited
miles of sleep around
us
Bumbling thru slumber
Blind numbers
In a tiled room
We sit & brood
Refuse to move
The guards refuse

and in the last place
and in the last sweet breath
& in stroke of side-wise crab

and in stars of plenty, stars of greed
in the written books & majesties
in fulfillment on a cliff
on the inside of butter
on smooth backs & camels
in the open vessel
in the vein
in lives untold who witnessed
                    everything

For those people who died
for Nirvana
for the heavenly creed
for you, for me

These lines are written
        to convey the message
To ignore the warning
To spree upward into
Tantalizing voices

To visit under-seas
Believe
Things more horrible
            than war
Things out of the tales
Great beasts
Suffering extinction

        •

Curses
Invocations

Weird bait-headed mongrels
I keep expecting one of you
to rise
Large buxom obese queens
garden hogs & cunt veterans
quaint cabbage saints
shit-hoarders & individualists
drag-strip officials

Tight-lipped losers
& lustful fuck salesmen
My militant dandies
all strange order of monsters
hot on the trail of the
woodvine
We welcome you to our
procession

•

All these monstrous
apologies
Words forsaken or
forgotten
loose walls falling
Tumbling down into
night. Fast friends,
earthly lovers, crash.
Sweet sorrow, blackness
falling soft rivers
of guilt on the
spilled roadside. Down
into fire, cry
down into silence

•

Argue w/breath
nice
while I cry
Midnight!

it must come
like dream
sperm
uncalled
from the center
Borderlands
where liquors
made
flow

it must come
unbidden
like the dawn
soft haste
No hurry
hairs curl

The phone rings

We create
the dawn

•

Stiff bundle breeding sorrow
Mare's milk

I fell in the earth
                & raped the snow
I got married to life
                & breathed w/my marrow
I saw young dancers
I am meat & need fuel
Need the whorey glimmer of tears
in women, all ages

Laughter sandwich, fuel
        for the lunch of meat minds
Now damn you, dance
Now dance
or die sleek & fat in your
reeking seats, still
buckled for flight

•

To have just come wondering
if the world is real is
sick to see the shape she's
made of. What wandering
lunacy have we soft created?

Certain no one meant it
sure someone started
Where is he?
Where is he or it when
        we need her?
Where are you?
In a flower?
In a flower?

To have just been born
        for beauty & see sadness
What is this frail sickness?

Now look. The chocolate bitch
        is in heat, bad bitch
for breeding
But we love her best

        •

If the writer can write, &
        the farmer can sow
Then all miracles concur,
        appear, & start happening
If the children eat, if their
        time of crying was Mid-
        Night

The earth needs them
soft dogs on the snow
Nestled in spring
When sun makes wine
& blood dances dangerous
        in the veins or vine

        •

The wild whore laughs
      like an ancient spinster
Crone, we see you, come again
      in the mind

I lie like fever

Dancing your nubile hush
willing to be possessed
      untold stories
      dare injuns rise
Trampled, like red-skins
      sacred fore-skin
Cancer began w/the knife's
      cruel blow & the damaged
rod has risen again
      in the East
          like a star
              on fire

•

Round-up, Rondolay, Rhonda,
Red, rich roll ruse rune
rake roan ran regard
if you know what I mean.
This is concrete imagery Vermont
The mouth leads this way
eye that way
No good faster the hand too slow
To exist in time we die/construct
prisms, prisons in a
void the truth faster these hang-ups
hold-ups shooting the republic
The president's dream behind
the throne
four-score fast fever the clinic
the wisdom syphilis doctor nurse
Indians Americans Atlantis
Save us guide us in time of need
prayer to the mind cell body
prayer to center of man prayer
to evening's last whisper as the
hand silently glides into peaceful
stones I await your coming
w/negligence   Speak to me!

don't leave me here alone Torture
clinic chamber I know the man
arrested   The stale bars his mother
who will help a match a cigarette
I'm going God What is your name

There must be some way to define
stop happening space shades
postures poses suspects The
World behind the word & all
insane utterance   Can't now
coming for us soon leave all over
The Republic is a big cross in a
big cross the nation The world on fire
Taxi from Africa   The Grand Hotel

He was drunk   a big party last
night there. Pastures fields
skunks snake invisible night birds
night hawks   summer disasters
out of doors listen to the lions
roar in the empty fields
of summer. These are forgotten
lands   Speak confidently of
the forest the end the joke
is on me   most certainly
There must be someone today who
knows what they do but they can't
Tell you   like feeding a child
Wine like sniffing Kotex
Cigars roar   field streams
blue babies lists   real estate
offices   word-vomit
mind soup crawling lice &

Tick bats, book bonds
Feeling streams lead to losers
back going back in all directions
sleeping these insane hours
I'll never wake up in a good mood
again.   I'm sick of these
stinky boots. Stories of animals
in the woods not stupid but
like Indians peeping out   their
little eyes in the night   I know
the forest & the evil moon tide.
"We sure look funny don't we fella?"

Plu-perfect. Forgotten. Songs
are good streams for a laugh.

The mind bird was a god fella
who minded labyrinths & lived in a well
He knew Jesus knew Newman knew
Me & Morganfield I hope you can
understand these last parables were
hope (less) Sure if you can regard
them as anything beyond matter surely
not more than twice fold fork follow
& loose-tree Now here's the rub rune

Rib-bait squalor the women of the quarter
yawned & meandered swimming dust
Tide for foodscapes to child-feed
No noon for misses The church called
bells inhabitants of the well come
To hell come to the bell funeral, jive
Negroes plenty fluttering their dark
smiles Mindless lepers con-men
The movie is popular this season in
all the hotels rich tourists from
the continent shore up & hold a story
Seance nightly the birds tell &
They know all Telephones crooks
& castanets the lines are wired
Listen hear those voices & all this
long distance from the other half
I love to hear ya ramble boy
missionary stallion. One day the
devil arrived only no tell or
you'll ruin the outcome He walked
to the pulpit & saved the city
while certainly scoring someone's
female daughter. When his cloak
was hoisted the snake was seen
& we all slipped back to lethargy.

Buildings gilded no interruptions.

Constructions everywhere. Our own house
was solid astrology Tiny flutes
won their starling's sunrise. And
in the estuary side-traps stopped
our dinner He came home w/bags
of meat & sacks of flour & the bread
rose & the family flourished.

●

And so I say to you
The silk handkerchief was
embroidered in China or Japan
behind the steel curtain   And
no one can cross the borderline
w/out proper credentials.
This is to say that we are all
sensate & occasionally sad
& if every partner in crime
were to incorporate promises
in his program the dance
might end & all our friends
would follow.

Who are our friends?

Are they sullen & slow? Do
they have great desire? Or
are they one of the multitude who
walk doubting their impossible
regret. Certainly things happen
& reoccur in continuous promise;
All of us have found a safe
niche where we can store up
riches & talk to our fellows
on the same premise of disaster.

But this will not do. No, this
will never do.   There are
continents & shores which
beseech our understanding.
Seldom have we been so slow.
Seldom have we been so far.

My only wish is to see
Far Arden again.

423

The truth is on his chest
The cellular excitement has
Totally inspired our magic
Veteran. And now for an
old trip.   I'm tired of thinking.

I want the old forms to
reassert their sexual cool.
My mind is just - you know.
And this morning before I sign
off I would like to tell you
about Texas Radio & the Big Beat.
It moves into the perimeter of
your sacred sincere & dedicated
Smile like a calm veteran
of the psychic war. He was
no general for he was not old.
He was no private for he
could not be told.
He was only a man & his
dedication extended to the last
degree. Poor pretentious soldier,
come home. The dark Los Angeles
evening is steaming the Church
that we attended & I miss
my boy. Stupid in green -
What the color green? When
I watch the T.V. & I see
helicopters swirling their
brutal & bountiful sensation
over the fields & the comic walls
I can only smile & fix a meal
& think about the child who
will one day own you.

In conclusion, darling, let
me repeat: your home is still
here, inviolate & certain
and I open the wide smile of
my remembrance. This to you
on the anniversary of our first
night. I know you love me
to talk this way. I hope
no one sees this message
written in the calm lonely
far out languid summer afternoon.
W/my total love [28]

•

the village recorder

1616 BUTLER AVENUE · WEST LOS ANGELES, CALIFORNIA 90025

ARTIST	JIM MORRISON		WORK ORDER NO.	958
CLIENT	ELECTRA		PURCHASE ORDER NO.	

STUDIO B	REEL 2 OF 4	DATE 12/8/2	TAPE MACHINE NO. MONO B	TAPE 96FA	EQ	SPEED
	PAGE 1 OF 2	O/D DATE	NO. OF TRACKS 1			15

☐ TONES AT H-T
☐ GOOD TAKES LEADERED
☐ GOOD TAKES MARKED
☐ GOOD TAKES AT HEAD OF REEL

CODE:
M - MASTER
NG - NO GOOD
PB - PLAYBACK
C - COMPLETE

O/D OVER DUB
FS - FALSE START
INT - INTERCUT
LFS - LONG FALSE START

ENGINEER JOHN HANEY

RECORD B. BIGSBY

TITLE	V.S.O.	TAKE NO.	CODE	TIME	TAKE NO.	CODE	TIME	TAKE NO.	CODE	TIME	TAKE NO.	CODE	TIME	TAKE NO.	CODE	TIME
(SONG) WHISKEY, MYSTICS, & MEN		1	C													
SING TO YOUR DADDY, IN YOUR HOUSE OF SUEDE		1	C													
SWEET SACRED MEAT		1	C													

TITLE	V.S.O.	TAKE NO.	CODE	TIME	TAKE NO.	CODE	TIME	TAKE NO.	CODE	TIME	TAKE NO.	CODE	TIME	TAKE NO.	CODE	TIME
CORRA'S SON/MESSANGER, ASIA		1	C													
		1	"													
PANTHER'S LIVING ROOM (SHORT)		1	C													
LISTEN TO THIS, WE IS STONED		1	C													

TITLE	V.S.O.	TAKE NO.	CODE	TIME	TAKE NO.	CODE	TIME	TAKE NO.	CODE	TIME	TAKE NO.	CODE	TIME	TAKE NO.	CODE	TIME
(LOUD) HELP, HELP, SAVE US FELLA		1	C	NG												
		2	C	HOLD												
DANCE, DANCE (SHORT)		1	C													

TITLE	V.S.O.	TAKE NO.	CODE	TIME	TAKE NO.	CODE	TIME	TAKE NO.	CODE	TIME	TAKE NO.	CODE	TIME	TAKE NO.	CODE	TIME
(INTRO SINGING) I'D LOVE TO STAY		1	C													
*(SONG PART) CAN YOU SEE, SELL ME YOUR PONY		1	C													

* MARKED PER ENG. INST.

the village
recorder

1616 BUTLER AVENUE · WEST LOS ANGELES, CALIFORNIA 90025

ARTIST	JIM MORRISON			WORK ORDER NO.	958
CLIENT	ELECTRA			PURCHASE ORDER NO.	

STUDIO	REEL 2 OF 4	DATE 12/8/70	TAPE MACHINE NO. MONO B	TAPE AGFA	EQ	SPEED
B	PAGE 2 OF 2	O/D DATE	NO. OF TRACKS 1			15

☐ TONES AT H-T ⊙	CODE:	O/D OVER DUB	ENGINEER JOHN HANEY
☐ GOOD TAKES LEADERED	M- MASTER	FS- FALSE START	
☐ GOOD TAKES MARKED	NG- NO GOOD	INT- INTERCUT	RECORD B. BIGSBY
☐ GOOD TAKES AT HEAD OF REEL	PB- PLAYBACK C- COMPLETE	LFS- LONG FALSE START	

TITLE				V.S.O.	TAKE NO.	CODE	TIME	TAKE NO.	CODE	TIME	TAKE NO.	CODE	TIME	TAKE NO.	CODE	TIME
1 PIANO	2 SOLO	3	4		1	FS		3	C	HOLD, TAMBORNE						
5	6	7	8		2	C										
9 TAMBORINE	10		12		1	FSC										
13	14	15	16		2	FS										

TITLE				V.S.O.	TAKE NO.	CODE	TIME	TAKE NO.	CODE	TIME	TAKE NO.	CODE	TIME	TAKE NO.	CODE	TIME
1 SIGH		3	4		1	C										
5 AWAKE, SHAKE DREAMS			8		1											
9 (ENGR. CUE "JIM,-....)		10									·					
13 POETRY		15	16		1	FS									·	

TITLE				V.S.O.	TAKE NO.	CODE	TIME	TAKE NO.	CODE	TIME	TAKE NO.	CODE	TIME	TAKE NO.	CODE	TIME
1	2	3	4													
5	6	7	8													
9	10	11	12													
13	14	15	16													

TITLE				V.S.O.	TAKE NO.	CODE	TIME	TAKE NO.	CODE	TIME	TAKE NO.	CODE	TIME	TAKE NO.	CODE	TIME
1	2	3	4													
5	6	7	8													
9	10	11	12													
13	14	15	16													

the village recorder

1616 BUTLER AVENUE • WEST LOS ANGELES, CALIFORNIA 90025

| ARTIST | JIM MORRISON | WORK ORDER NO. | 958 |
| CLIENT | ELECTRA | PURCHASE ORDER NO. | |

| STUDIO | REEL 3 OF 4 | DATE 12/8/70 | TAPE MACHINE NO. MONO "B" | TAPE AGFA | EQ | SPEED |
| B | PAGE 1 OF | O/D DATE | NO. OF TRACKS MONO | | | 15 |

☐ TONES AT H-T ⓐ ⓑ	CODE:		O/D · OVER DUB	ENGINEER JOHN HANBY
☐ GOOD TAKES LEADERED	M · MASTER		FS · FALSE START	
☐ GOOD TAKES MARKED	NG · NO GOOD		INT · INTERCUT	RECORD B. BIGSBY
☐ GOOD TAKES AT HEAD OF REEL	PB · PLAYBACK		LFS · LONG FALSE	
	C · COMPLETE		START	

TITLE	V.S.O.	TAKE NO.	CODE	TIME	TAKE NO.	CODE	TIME	TAKE NO.	CODE	TIME	TAKE NO.	CODE	TIME
(POETRY) AWARE, SHAKE DOWN		1	C										
(ENGR. CUE "STEP BACK"...)													
(TAMBORINE INTRO)		1	C										
IN THE TILED ROOM, FUCK SALEMAN		2											

TITLE	V.S.O.	TAKE NO.	CODE	TIME	TAKE NO.	CODE	TIME	TAKE NO.	CODE	TIME	TAKE NO.	CODE	TIME
WHAT WANDERING LUNACY HAVE WE CREATED —		1	C										
IF THE WRITER CAN WRITE —		1	C										
STAR ON FIRE —		1	C										

TITLE	V.S.O.	TAKE NO.	CODE	TIME	TAKE NO.	CODE	TIME	TAKE NO.	CODE	TIME	TAKE NO.	CODE	TIME
(SLATED — "YOU'RE ON")													
RONDA (& OTHER 'R's) (LONG)		1	C										
(SLATED "JIM, FORGET THAT MIC")													
SHORT POEM —		1	C										
(SLATED "READY")													

TITLE "LETTER TO A SOLDIER	V.S.O.	TAKE NO.	CODE	TIME	TAKE NO.	CODE	TIME	TAKE NO.	CODE	TIME	TAKE NO.	CODE	TIME
(AND SO I SAID TO YOU,		1	C										
IN CONCLUSION, DARLING,													
WITH													

LONG

the village recorder

1616 BUTLER AVENUE • WEST LOS ANGELES, CALIFORNIA 90025

ARTIST	JIM MORRISON						WORK ORDER NO.	958		

CLIENT	ELECTRA						PURCHASE ORDER NO.			

STUDIO B	REEL 4 of 4	DATE 12/8/70	TAPE MAC(MONO) MONO "B"	TAPE AGFA	EQ	SPEED 15
	PAGE 1 of	O/D DATE	NO. OF TRACKS MONO	ENGINEER JOHN HANEY		

☐ TONES AT H-T   ⊕   ⊕
☐ GOOD TAKES LEADERED
☐ GOOD TAKES MARKED
☐ GOOD TAKES AT HEAD OF REEL

CODE:
M - MASTER
NG - NO GOOD
PB - PLAYBACK
C - COMPLETE

O/D - OVER DUB
FS - FALSE START
INT - INTERCUT
LFS - LONG FALSE START

RECORD **B. BIGSBY**

TITLE TAMBORINE (INTRO)	V.S.O.	TAKE NO.	CODE	TIME	TAKE NO.	CODE	TIME	TAKE NO.	CODE	TIME	TAKE NO.	CODE	TIME	TAKE NO.	CODE	TIME
1 (SLATED "READY")	4															
5 IMPROVISATIONS	8															
9 "WELL YOU KNOW I GOT A 10	12															
13 LOT A THINGS TO TELL YOU BABY" I C																

TITLE ("FRANK'S COOL")	V.S.O.	TAKE NO.	CODE	TIME	TAKE NO.	CODE	TIME	TAKE NO.	CODE	TIME	TAKE NO.	CODE	TIME	TAKE NO.	CODE	TIME
1 2	3 4															
5 GIRLS PART	8															
9 (RAP & PREPORATION & 3 FS) 10	12															
13 POEM AS FAR AS "NICHE"																

TITLE POEM " " " "	V.S.O.	TAKE NO.	CODE	TIME	TAKE NO.	CODE	TIME	TAKE NO.	CODE	TIME	TAKE NO.	CODE	TIME	TAKE NO.	CODE	TIME
1 READY	3 4															
5 6	7 8															
9 10	11 12															
13 14	15 16															

TITLE	V.S.O.	TAKE NO.	CODE	TIME	TAKE NO.	CODE	TIME	TAKE NO.	CODE	TIME	TAKE NO.	CODE	TIME	TAKE NO.	CODE	TIME
1 2	3 4															
5 6	7 8															
9 10	11 12															
13 14	15 16															

FILM
TREATMENT

THE HITCHIKER

A film idea by Jim Morrison

THE SCREEN IS BLACK.   We hear a young man's voice in
casual conversation with friends.

>   No, this guy told me you can go down
>   across the border and buy a girl
>   and bring her back and that's what
>   I'm goin' to do, I'm gonna go down
>   there and buy one of them and bring
>   her back and marry her. I am.

An older woman's voice

>   Billy, are you completely crazy?

We hear the good-natured laughter of the woman, a man,
and another friend as Billy's insistent voice rises
through saying

>   BILLY

>   No, it's true. Really. This guy
>   told me. It's true. I'm really
>   gonna do it.

The film changes to COLOR. A couple sit at a small
table in a simulated border town night club. It is
a CLOSE shot, reminding us possibly of Picasso's
"Absinthe Drinkers." The atmosphere is suggested by
peripheral sounds such as boisterous young voices,
curses in a foreign language, the tinkling of glasses
and music from a small rock band. Perhaps a dancer
is visible in the background. Perhaps topless. An
anonymous waitress could enter the frame and leave,
serving drinks.

The HERO is drunk and he's trying to persuade an
attractive Mexican girl, a waitress in the bar, a
whore, to cross the border and marry him. The girl
tolerates him. She is working, hustling drinks, and
has to listen but also she likes him. In some way, he
interests her.

>   BILLY

>   I bet the only reason you won't come
>   with me is because I ain't got any
>   money. Well, listen. I'm tellin' you.

435

I'm gonna go back up there and get
me some money, lots of it, maybe
even ten thousand. And then I'm
comin' back for you. I'm comin' back.

He weaves off screen, determined, drunk, camera holds
on girl, smiling, wistfully and ironically after him.
Then she grabs another young American and pulls him
down beside her.

THE GIRL

Hey, man, you want to buy me a drink?

TITLE

THE HITCHHIKER

(An American Pastoral)

Film changes to BLACK and WHITE. It is dawn on the
American desert; it's cold, and he stands hunched in
his jacket, by the side of the highway. The sun is
rising. We hold on him as a few cars go by at long
intervals. We hear the car coming, watch his eyes
watching, he sticks his thumb out. CUT TO profile
shot, as a car swishes by. The third car stops and he
runs, not too energetically and gets inside.

INTERIOR car. Middle-aged man in a business suit. He
asks the hitchhiker where he is goin'.

BILLY
(mumbling)

LA.

He is obviously reluctant to do any talking.

THE DRIVER

I can take you as far as Amarillo and
then you'll have to go on from there.

BILLY

(No reply. No recognition.)

436

DRIVER

What are you going to do when you get
to LA? Have you got a job lined up?

BILLY
(No answer. He is beginning to nod.)

The man drives on. We see glimpses of the American
landscape out the window of the car. The man glances
sideways occasionally at Billy who is sleeping.

CLOSE UP of the man's right hand moving snake-like
towards the hiker's left leg. He hesitates and then
touches it above the knee. Immediately, a 38 revolver
appears from Billy's jacket and points at the driver.

BILLY
Pull over.

Profile of car, left side, extreme long shot. We
hear a shot. The hitchhiker comes around the rear of
the car, opens the door, and pulls the driver toward
camera, his corpse that is, to the gully, and, after
stripping his wallet of all the cash, gets into the car
and drives away.

The kid is standing beside the car with his thumb out.
The hood is raised. The engine has failed. A State
Patrolman (we learn this from his uniform, western hat,
and badge) stops in his own un-marked car. Billy gets
in the car. The sheriff is friendly. He talks a lot.
He tells Billy that he's just getting back home after
delivering two lunatics from his local jail to the
state asylum.

SHERIFF

I had to put them both in straight
jackets and throw them in the back
of the wagon. I had to. They were
totally uninhibited. I mean, if
I let 'em loose, they just start
jerking off and playing with each
other, so I had to keep them tied up.

The killer is trying to stay awake. He's strung out
on bennies, and also just plain exhausted, and he's
fighting to follow the man's conversation. The sheriff
rambles on. Billy is in that weird state between sleep
and waking where it is hard to distinguish between
what's being said in reality and what he hears in
his dream. The sheriff asks a question. He answers
and then jerks up suddenly to realize that he's been
inventing his own dialogue inside his head. Finally,
he can take it no longer. He pulls the gun out and
orders the sheriff to pull over to the side of the
road. Then he forces him to unlock the trunk, orders
him inside and slams the lid.

INTERIOR of car. The hitchhiker is driving on.

As the car slows down for an upgrade, the trunk flies
open and the sheriff tumbles out into the dust.
Billy sees it in the rear view mirror. He slams on the
brakes, jumps out of the car and runs back to the spot.
From off in the desert, we see the sheriff racing
insanely toward the camera. He suddenly leaps and
throws himself flat on the ground behind a sand dune,
next to the camera. From this point of view,
the sheriff crouched and breathing in heavy gasps, we
watch the kid stand on the side of the road, stare out
into the desert and finally get back into the car and
drive away.

Billy is hitchhiking again. Obviously, he has ditched
the sheriff's car somewhere along the way. A car pulls
over. There is a young man driving and, in the back
seat, are his wife and two small children, a boy and
a girl. The driver is friendly, tells him he used to
hitchhike a lot himself and volunteers the information
that he has just returned home from two years in Viet
Nam, where he was a pilot. Billy pulls out the gun
and lets them know immediately that he wants them to
take him anywhere he wants to go. Otherwise, he'll
kill them.

It is NIGHT. They pull into a gas station. Billy
is hungry, so are the kids. So he goes with the ex-
aviator into a small country store that's part of the
station. He warns the family to keep quiet or he'll
kill everyone.

INSIDE the country store. A seedy old man behind the
counter. They ask him for a bunch of ham sandwiches.
In close-up, we watch him slice the meat, the knife
hesitating minutely, deciding on the thickness of
each slice. The two men stand there watching him.
Suddenly, the husband wheels around and gets a grip on
the hitchhiker from behind. They whirl madly around
the store, the father screaming for the proprietor to
call the police.

THE MAN

> Stop him! He's got a gun!! He's
> gonna kill us!!! Help me!!!!

Billy somehow manages to get his gun out and forces
the man to the car. The store owner stares after him,
mouth agape, then picks up the receiver to call the
police.

MORNING. A young boy finds the car, pulled off on
a side road, splattered with blood. He opens the door
and the little girl's baby doll, the naked, flesh-
colored rubber kind, and in close-up, we see blood
on it.

The EXTERIOR of a run-down shack in the country.
We hear the sounds from inside. INTERIOR of
shack. Television and radio and newspaper reporters
including an attractive woman with a notebook, are
interviewing the killer's father. He's a very old
man, an alcoholic, who is slightly pleased to be
thrust suddenly into the spotlight, but who treats the
situation with a grave sense of public image and
self-irony.

THE FATHER

> He was always a pretty strange boy,
> specially after his mother passed
> away. Then he got real quiet. He
> didn't have many friends. Just his
> brothers and sisters.

GIRL REPORTER

> Mr. Cooke, is there anything you'd
> like to tell your son?

FATHER

> Yes, there is. Billy, if you can
> hear me, son, please turn yourself
> in. Cause what you're doin', it
> just ain't right. You're not doin'
> right, son. And you know it.

During this appeal, the camera has moved slowly into a
CLOSE UP of the old man's face.

INTERIOR. Car. Night. Rain. A car radio. The light
glows yellow in the dark car. The radio is playing a
country gospel hour. A revival meeting. The preacher
and his flock. As Billy listens, we flash back into
his past, over the rain and windshield wipers. We see
an old man and a young boy in the woods. The man is
Billy's father and the boy is Billy himself at about
age seven or eight. The father teaches his son how to
shoot a gun. He tells him to aim at a rabbit.

THE FATHER

> Don't be afraid, son. Don't be
> afraid. Just squeeze one off.

We see a rabbit pinioned in a rifle's telescopic sight.

A small town high school, 3:30, bell rings, school is
out. The kids gush from the building and flow like a
human stream to the favorite drive-in restaurant.

INTERIOR of car. Billy is eating a cheeseburger and
coke. Through his windows he watches the movements of
one of the car hops. She is wearing slacks and with
him we watch her ass and thighs. When she comes to
collect, he asks her to come for a ride with him. We
hear him say this but the ensuing dialogue is shown in
pantomime. The actual voices are drowned out by the
sounds of radios, kids talking.

440

They are driving up a mountain road. The Rolling Stones' "I Can't Get No Satisfaction" comes on the radio. Billy sings along with the record with wild abandon and squirms in his seat like a toad.

The car is parked on a rocky view overlooking the ocean. He gets out of the car and dances around it, acting crazy, and howling like an Indian. He ducks up and down appearing and re-appearing in different windows. She laughs at his clowning.

The couple are in the back seat, vaguely we see their movements, hear them whispering, laughing, talking. CUT TO outside of car. They get out of the back of the car, hair and clothes disarranged and move side by side into a rough terrain behind some rocks. Camera holds on the rocks. A primeval rock formation. At a rhythm that is peculiarly excruciating, we hear three gunshots.

A restroom in an LA service station. EXTERIOR. Billy enters restroom.

INTERIOR restroom. Billy shaves with soap in restroom mirror, runs his wet hands through his hair.

EXTERIOR, downtown LA. Camera follows him from a car, as he wanders through the downtown crowds of Broadway and Main Street. Many times he is lost to our view. We see him in an arcade, where he plays a pinball machine.

CLOSE-UP of pinball game in progress.

Billy in photo booth. Flash of the lights.

CLOSE-UP of four automatic photos: flash flash flash flash. Four faces of Billy.

Billy in downtown hamburger stand. He is eating, seen from behind, Gun enters frame left. He turns and sees it, stares back blankly.

CUT TO EXTERIOR, street. In hand-held confused close-up sequence, we see him dragged and shoved into the back seat of a car (Police car). He is kicked and beaten. During the struggle, we hear many men's voices, gloating righteous exclamations.

MEN

> So you're the little bastard that
> killed all those people! (Kick)
> You had a good time, didn't you? (Kick)
> You really killed 'em, didn't you?

Hands cuffed behind his back, he looks up with a
confused expression and says:

BILLY

> But I'm a good boy.

The men laugh.

Film switches to COLOR. A montage of extant
photographs representing death. The body of Che
Guevara, a northern renaissance Dutch crucifixion,
bullfight, slaughter house, mandalas and into
abstraction. A nature film, of a mongoose killing a
cobra, a black dog runs free on the beach. FADE INTO
BLACKNESS.

442   EXTERIOR night. On the steps of City Hall of Justice
we see the hitchhiker descend dream-like in slow
motion, move languorously across a deserted city square
toward the camera until he covers the lens and seems to
pass through it.

Seen now from behind, as he moves away from lens, he
enters a desert outskirts region where he finds an
automobile grave yard. He is wandering in Eternity.
In the junkyard, three people squat around a small
fire. They're cooking potatoes in the coals, an older
man named DOC pokes the fire with a stick. There is
an older woman, funky, glamorous, and the third person
is a young boy, a mute, of indeterminate age. He is
slightly made up with white make-up. They are hoboes
in Eternity and are not surprised to see him. He nears
the fire.

DOC

> Well, how ya doin', kid? I see you
> did it again. Ya hungry? There's
> some food here, if ya want it.

Billy doesn't speak. He stares at the moon. The woman
has kept her head down, her hair covering her face.

                    DOC

     Billy's back. Blue Lady, didja hear
     me? I said Billy's back.

She looks up for the first time.

                 BLUE LADY

     Hi, Billy.

                   BILLY

     Hello, Blue Lady.

He looks at the boy.

     Hiya, Clown Boy.

CLOWN BOY claps his hands and nods, his face,
contorted grotesquely in greeting. They sit for
awhile like this, and stare at the fire. They eat the   **443**
potatoes. Then Doc rises and says:

                    DOC

     The sun's gonna be up in a while. I
     guess we'd better move on.

Slowly, one by one, the other two rise. Doc puts out
the fire with dirt and says:

                    DOC

     Ya comin' with us, Billy?

                   BILLY
                (thinking hard)

     I don't know, Doc, I just don't
     know.

Doc smiles.

                              DOC

          Well, we'll see ya later, kid. The
                    rest of the gang will be real
glad
          to see ya. They sure will. Well...

Doc, Clown Boy and the Blue Lady start moving toward
the rising sun into the mountain desert. Every now and
then, they turn and wave, Clown Boy leaping up and down
madly and waving goodbye.

As they slowly disappear, camera changes focus to
Billy, the hitchhiker, the kid, the killer, hunkered
over the dead smoldering fire.

                    THE END[29]

444

I'm interested in film because to me it's the closest approximation in art that we have to the actual flow of consciousness, in both dreamlife and in the everyday perception of the world.[30]

IV

LYRICS

BREAK ON THROUGH

You know the day destroys
    the night
Night divides the day
Tried to run
Tried to hide
Break on through to the other side
Break on through to the other side
Break on through to the other side

We chased our pleasures here
Dug our treasures there
Can you still recall
The time we cried?
Break on through to the other side
Break on through to the other side
Break on through to the other side

Everybody loves my baby
Everybody loves my baby

She get high, she get high
She get high, she get high

I found an island in your arms
A country in your eyes
Arms that chain
Eyes that lied
Break on through to the other side
Break on through to the other side
Break on through to the other side

Made the scene from week to week
Day to day, hour to hour
The gate is straight
Deep and wide
Break on through to the other side
Break on through to the other side
Break on through, break on
    through
Break on through, break on
    through[31] [32]

SOUL KITCHEN

Well, the clock says it's time to
    close now
I guess I'd better go now
I'd really like to stay here all night

The cars crawl past all stuffed
    with eyes
Street lights shed their hollow glow
Your brain seems bruised with
    numb surprise

Still one place to go
Still one place to go

Let me sleep all night in your
    soul kitchen
Warm my mind near your gentle
    stove
Turn me out and I'll wander, baby
Stumbling in the neon groves

Your fingers weave quick minarets
Speaking secret alphabets
I light another cigarette
Learn to forget, learn to forget
Learn to forget, learn to forget

Let me sleep all night in your
    soul kitchen
Warm my mind near your gentle
    stove
Turn me out and I'll wander, baby
Stumbling in the neon groves

Well, the clock says it's time to
    close now
I know I have to go now,
I really want to stay here all night
All night
All night

THE CRYSTAL SHIP

Before you slip into
    unconsciousness
I'd like to have another kiss
Another flashing chance at bliss
Another kiss
Another kiss

The days are bright and filled
    with pain
Enclose me in your gentle rain
The time you ran was too insane
We'll meet again
We'll meet again

Oh, tell me where your freedom lies
The streets are fields that never die
Deliver me from reasons why
You'd rather cry
I'd rather fly.

The crystal ship is being filled
A thousand girls, a thousand thrills
A million ways to spend your time
When we get back
I'll drop a line

TWENTIETH CENTURY FOX

Well, she's fashionably lean
And she's fashionably late
She'll never rank a scene
She'll never break a date
But she's no drag
Just watch the way she walks

She's a twentieth century fox
She's a twentieth century fox
No tears, no fears
No ruined years
No clocks
She's a twentieth century fox

She's the queen of cool
And she's the lady who waits
Since her mind left school
It never hesitates
She won't waste time
On elementary talk

'Cause she's a twentieth
    century fox
She's a twentieth century fox
Got the world locked up
Inside a plastic box
She's a twentieth century fox
Twentieth century fox
She's a twentieth century fox

I LOOKED AT YOU

I looked at you
You looked at me
I smiled at you
You smiled at me

And we're on our way
No, we can't turn back
Yeah, we're on our way
And we can't turn back
'Cause it's too late
Too late, too late
Too late, too late
And we're on our way
No, we can't turn back
Yeah, we're on our way
And we can't turn back

I walk with you
You walk with me
I talk to you
You talk to me

And we're on our way
No, we can't turn back
Yeah, we're on our way
And we can't turn back
'Cause it's too late
Too late, too late
Too late, too late

Take the Hiway to The
                    End of the Night
                        (end of the night (2)
Take a Journey to the
                    Bright Midnight
                        (end of the Night (2)

Hold on tight
          (while we)
                Fall Thru the Night (2)

Hold on tight
Hold on Tight
Hold on Tight
Hold on Tight

Its time to ignite
The Carnival lights
Try to set the night on Fire

Learn to explore
Beyond the door
Try to set the night on Fire

Take the highway to the end of
    the night
End of the night
End of the night
Take a journey to the bright
    midnight
End of the night
End of the night

Realms of bliss
Realms of light
Some are born to sweet delight
Some are born to sweet delight
Some are born to the endless night

End of the night
End of the night
End of the night
End of the night

Time to live
Time to lie
Time to laugh
Time to die

Take it easy, baby
Take it as it comes
Don't move too fast
If you want your love to last
You've been movin' much too fast

Time to walk
Time to run
Time to aim your arrows
At the sun

Take it easy, baby
Take it as it comes
Don't move too fast
If you want your love to last
You've been movin' much too fast

Go real slow
You'll like it more and more
Take it as it comes
Specialize in havin' fun

Take it easy, baby
Take it as it comes
Don't move too fast
If you want your love to last
You've been movin' much too fast
Movin' much too fast
Movin' much too fast

473

THE END

This is the end, beautiful friend
This is the end, my only friend
The end of our elaborate plans
The end of everything that stands
The end

No safety or surprise
The end
I'll never look into your eyes again

Can you picture what will be
So limitless and free
Desperately in need of some
   stranger's hand
In a desperate land

Lost in a Roman wilderness of pain,
And all the children are insane
All the children are insane
Waiting for the summer rain

There's danger on the edge of town
Ride the King's highway
Weird scenes inside the gold mine
Ride the highway West, baby

Ride the snake
Ride the snake
To the lake
To the lake

The ancient lake, baby
The snake is long
Seven miles
Ride the snake

He's old
And his skin is cold
The West is the best
The West is the best
Get here and we'll do the rest

The blue bus is calling us
The blue bus is calling us
Driver, where you taking us?

The killer awoke before dawn
He put his boots on
He took a face from the
   ancient gallery
And he walked on down the hall

He went into the room where
   his sister lived
And then he paid a visit to
   his brother
And then he walked on down
   the hall
And he came to a door
And he looked inside
"Father?"
"Yes, son?"
"I want to kill you.
"Mother, I want to. . . . . ."

Come on, baby, take a chance
   with us
Come on, baby, take a chance
   with us
Come on, baby, take a chance
   with us
And meet me at the back of the
   blue bus.
This is the end, beautiful friend
This is the end, my only friend
The end

It hurts to set you free
But you'll never follow me

The end of laughter and soft lies
The end of nights we tried to die

This is the end

476

Strange days have found us
Strange days have tracked us down
~~they're~~ they're going to destroy
~~~~ our casual joys
we shall go on playing or find a new town

strange eyes fill strange rooms
voices will signal their tired end
The hostess is grinning
Her guests sleep from sinning
Hear me talk of sin you know this is it

Strange days have found us
And thru their strange hours we linger alone
our bodies confused
Memories misused
~~~~ we run from the day
        to a strange night of stone

From
Strange Days
September 1967

Strange days have found us
Strange days have tracked us down
They're goin' to destroy
Our casual joys
We shall go on playing
Or find a new town

Strange eyes fill strange rooms
Voices will signal their tired end
The hostess is grinning
Her guests sleep from sinning
Hear me talk of sin and
You know this is it

Strange days have found us
And through their strange hours
We linger alone
Bodies confused
Memories misused
As we run from the day
To a strange night of stone

Unhappy girl
Left all alone
Playin' solitaire
Playin' warden to your soul
You are locked in a prison
Of your own devise
And you can't believe
What it does to me
To see you cryin'

Unhappy girl
Tear your web away
Saw thru all your bars
Melt your cell today
You are caught in a prison
Of your own devise

Unhappy girl
Fly fast away
Don't miss your chance
To swim in mystery
You are dying in a prison
Of your own devise

Let's swim to the moon
Let's climb thru the tide
Penetrate the evening
That the city sleeps to hide

Let's swim out tonight, love
It's our turn to try
Parked beside the ocean
On our moonlight drive

Let's swim to the moon
Let's climb thru the tide
Surrender to the waiting worlds
That lap against our side

Nothin' left open
And no time to decide
We've stepped into a river
On our moonlight drive

Let's swim to the moon
Let's climb thru the tide
You reach a hand to hold me
But I can't be your guide

Easy, I love you as I watch you glide
Falling thru wet forests
On our moonlight drive
Moonlight drive

C'mon, baby, gonna take a
    little ride
Goin' down by the ocean side
Gonna get real close
Get real tight
Baby, gonna drown tonight
Goin' down, down, down

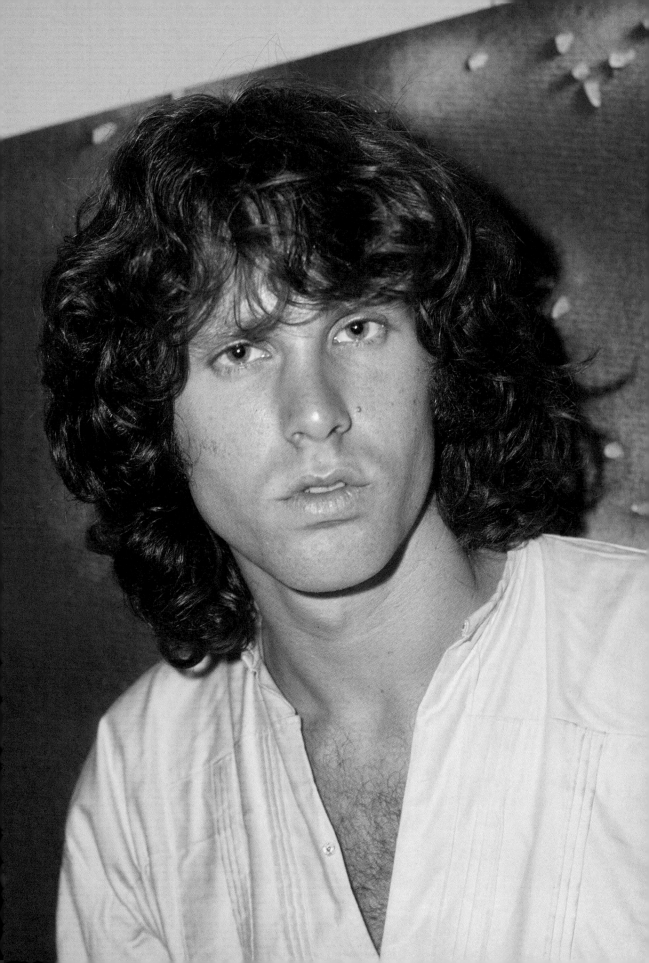

PEOPLE ARE STRANGE

People are strange
When you're a stranger
Faces look ugly
When you're alone
Women seem wicked
When you're unwanted
Streets are uneven
When you're down

When you're strange
Faces come out of the rain
When you're strange
No one remembers your name
When you're strange
When you're strange
When you're strange

MY EYES HAVE SEEN YOU

My eyes have seen you
My eyes have seen you
My eyes have seen you
Stand in your door
Meet inside
Show me some more
Show me some more
Show me some more

My eyes have seen you
My eyes have seen you
My eyes have seen you
Turn and stare
Fix your hair
Move upstairs
Move upstairs
Move upstairs

My eyes have seen you
My eyes have seen you
My eyes have seen you
Free from disguise
Gazing on a city
Under television skies
Television skies
Television skies

My eyes have seen you
My eyes have seen you
My eyes have seen you
Let them photograph your soul
Memorize your alleys
On an endless roll
Endless roll
Endless roll
Endless roll

I CAN'T SEE YOUR FACE IN MY MIND

I can't see your face in my mind
I can't see your face in my mind
Carnival dogs consume the lines
Can't see your face in my mind

Don't you cry
Baby, please don't cry
And don't look at me with
     your eyes

I can't seem to find the right lie
I can't seem to find the right lie
Insanity's horse adorns the sky
Can't seem to find the right lie

Carnival dogs consume the lines
Can't see your face in my mind

Don't you cry
Baby, please don't cry
I won't need your picture
Until we say goodbye

488

WHEN THE MUSIC'S OVER

When the music's over
When the music's over here
When the music's over
Turn out the lights
Turn out the lights
Turn out the lights

When the music's over
When the music's over
When the music's over
Turn out the lights
Turn out the lights
Turn out the lights

For the music is your special friend
Dance on fire as it intends
Music is your only friend
Until the end
Until the end
Until the end

Cancel my subscription
to the Resurrection
Send my credentials
to the house of detention
I got some friends inside

The face in the mirror won't stop
The girl in the window won't drop
A feast of friends
Alive she cried
Waiting for me outside

Before I sink into the big sleep
I want to hear
I want to hear
The scream of the butterfly

Come back, baby
Back into my arms
We're getting tired of hangin'
    around
Waiting around
With our heads to the ground
I hear a very gentle sound
Very near, yet very far
Very soft, yet very clear
Come today
Come today

What have they done to the earth?
What have they done to our
    fair sister?
Ravaged and plundered
And ripped her
And bit her
Stuck her with knives
In the side of the dawn
And tied her with fences
And dragged her down

I hear a very gentle sound
With your ear down to the ground
We want the world and we want it
We want the world and we want it,
    now
Now? NOW!

Persian night, babe!
See the light, babe!
Save us! Jesus! Save us!

So when the music's over
When the music's over here
When the music's over
Turn out the lights
Turn out the lights
Turn out the lights

For the music is your special friend
Dance on fire as it intends
Music is your only friend
Until the end
Until the end
Until the end

HELLO, I LOVE YOU

Hello, I love you
Won't you tell me your name?
Hello, I love you
Let me jump in your game
Hello, I love you
Won't you tell me your name?
Hello, I love you
Let me jump in your game

She's walkin' down the street
Blind to every eye she meets
Do you think you'll be the guy
To make the queen of the angels
    sigh?

Hello, I love you
Won't you tell me your name?
Hello, I love you
Let me jump in your game
Hello, I love you
Won't you tell me your name?
Hello, I love you
Let me jump in your game

She holds her head so high
Like a statue in the sky
Her arms are wicked
And her legs are long
When she moves
My brain screams out this song

Sidewalk crouches at her feet
Like a dog that begs
For something sweet
Do you hope to make her see you,
    fool?
Do you hope to pluck this dusky
    jewel?

Hello, Hello, Hello, Hello, Hello,
Hello, Hello
I want you
I need my baby
Love, Love
Hello, Hello, Hello

LOVE STREET

She lives on Love Street
Lingers long on Love Street
She has a house and garden
I would like to see what happens

She has robes and she has monkeys
Lazy diamond studded flunkies
She has wisdom and knows what
   to do
She has me and she has you

She has wisdom and knows what
   to do
She has me and she has you

I see you live on Love Street
There's the store where the
   creatures meet
I wonder what they do in there
Summer Sunday and a year
I guess I like it fine, so far

She lives on Love Street
Lingers long on Love Street
She has a house and garden
I would like to see what happens

NOT TO TOUCH THE EARTH

Not to touch the earth
Not to see the sun
Nothing left to do
But run, run, run
Let's run
Let's run

House upon the hill
Moon is lying still
Shadows of the trees
Witnessing the wild breeze
Come on, baby, run with me
Let's run

Run with me
Run with me
Run with me
Let's run

The mansion is warm at the top of
   the hill
Rich are the rooms and the
   comforts there
Red are the arms of luxuriant chairs
And you won't know a thing till
   you get inside

Dead President's corpse in the
   driver's car
The engine runs on glue and tar
Come on along, not going very far
To the East to meet the Czar

Run with me
Run with me
Run with me
Let's run

Some outlaws live by the side of
   a lake
The minister's daughter's in love
   with the snake
Who lives in a well by the side of
   the road
Wake up, girl, we're almost home
We should see the gates by morning
We should be inside by evening

Sun, sun, sun
Burn, burn, burn
Soon, soon, soon
Moon, moon, moon
I will get you
Soon
Soon
Soon

I am the Lizard King
I can do anything

SUMMER'S ALMOST GONE

Summer's almost gone
Summer's almost gone
Almost gone
Yeah
It's almost gone

Where will we be
When the summer's gone?

Morning found us calmly unaware
Noon burned gold into our hair
At night we swam the laughing sea

When summer's gone
Where will we be?
Where will we be?
Where will we be?

Morning found us calmly unaware
Noon burned gold into our hair
At night we swam the laughing sea

When summer's gone
Where will we be?

Summer's almost gone
Summer's almost gone
We had some good times
But they're gone
The winter's coming on
Summer's almost gone

THE UNKNOWN SOLDIER

Wait until the war is over
And we're both a little older
The unknown soldier

Breakfast where the news is read
Television children fed
Unborn, living
Living, dead
Bullet strikes the helmet's head

And it's all over
For the unknown soldier
It's all over
For the unknown soldier

"Company halt!"

"Present arms!"

Make a grave for the unknown
    soldier
Nestled in your hollow shoulder
The unknown soldier

Breakfast where the news is read
Television children fed
Bullet strikes the helmet's head

And it's all over, the war is over
It's all over, war is over
It's all over, baby,
All over, baby!

My wild love went riding
She rode all the day
She wrote to the devil
And asked him to pay

The devil was wiser
It's time to repent
He asked her to give back
The money she spent

My wild love went riding
She rode to the sea
She gathered together
Some shells for her hair

She rode and she rode on
She rode for a while
Then stopped for an evening
And laid her head down

She rode on to Christmas
She rode to the farm
She rode to Japan
And re-entered a town

By this time the weather
Had changed one degree
She asked for the people
To let her go free

My wild love is crazy
She screams like a bird
She moans like a cat
When she wants to be heard

My wild love went riding
She rode for an hour
She rode and she rested
And then she rode on

We could be so good together
Yeah, so good together
We could be so good together
Yeah, we could
I know we could

Tell you lies
I'll tell you wicked lies
Tell you lies
Tell you wicked lies

I'll tell you 'bout the world that
    we'll invent
Wanton world without lament
Enterprise, expedition
Invitation and invention

Yeah, so good together
Ah, so good together
We could be so good together
Yeah, we could
I know we could

We could be so good together
Yeah, so good together
We could be so good together
Yeah, we could
I know we could

Tell you lies
Tell you wicked lies
Tell you lies
Tell you wicked lies

The time you wait subtracts
    from joy
Beheads the angels you destroy
Angels fight, angels cry
Angels dance and angels die

Yeah, so good together
Ah, so good together
We could be so good together
Yeah, we could
I know we could

496

FIVE TO ONE

Five to one, baby
One in five
No one here gets out alive now
You get yours, baby
I'll get mine
Gonna make it, baby
If we try

The old get old and the young
    get stronger
May take a week and it may take
    longer
They got the guns but we got
    the numbers

Gonna win, yeah we're takin' over
Come on!

Your ballroom days are over, baby
Night is drawing near
Shadows of the evening
Crawl across the years
You walk across the floor
With a flower in your hand
Trying to tell me no one
    understands
Trade in your hours for a handful
    of dimes
Gonna make it baby, in our prime
Get together one more time (10x)

Well, c'mon, honey
Get along home and wait for me
Baby, I'll be home in just a little
    while
Y'see, I gotta go out in this car with
    these people
And get fucked up

Get together one more time
Get together one more time
Get together, gotta get together
Gotta get together
Got to take you up on the
    mountains

Love my girl, she's lookin' good
Lookin' real good
C'mon love ya
Feel, hey
Come on

My wild love went riding
she rode all the day
She rode to the devil
& asked him to pay

The devil was wiser
its time to repent
He asked her to give back
the money he spent

My wild love went riding
She rode to the sea
She gathered together
some shells for her hair

She rode & she rode on
She rode for a while
Then stopped for an evening
& laid her head down

She rode on to Christmas
She rode to the farm
She rode to Japan
& re-entered a Town

By this time the weather
had changed one degree
She asked for the people
To let her go free

SHAMAN'S BLUES

There will never be another one
    like you
There will never be another one
    who can
Do the things you do, oh
Will you give another chance?
Will you try a little try?
Please stop and you'll remember
We were together, anyway

All right!

And if you have a certain evening
You could lend to me
I'd give it all right back to you
Know how it has to be, with you
I know your moods
And your mind
And your mind
And your mind
And your mind
And your mind
And your mind
And you're mine

Will you stop and think and wonder
Just what you'll see
Out on the train-yard
Nursing penitentiary
It's gone, I cry, out long

Did you stop to consider
How it will feel
Cold grinding grizzly bear jaws
Hot on your heels

Do you often stop and whisper
In Saturday's shore
The whole world's a savior
Who could ever, ever, ever, ever,
    ever, ever
Ask for more?
Do you remember?
Will you stop
Will you stop the pain?

There will never be another one
 like you
There will never be another one
 who can
Do the things you do, oh
Will you give another chance?
Will you try a little try?
Please stop and you'll remember
We were together, anyway

All right!

How you must think and wonder
How I must feel
Out on the meadows
While you're on the field
I'm alone for you
And I cry

"He's sweatin', look at him . . .
Optical promise . . .
You'll be dead and in hell before
 I'm born . . .
sure thing. . .bridesmaid. . .
The only solution. . .
Isn't it amazing?"

DO IT

Please me
Please me, babe
Please me

Please, please listen to me children
Please, please listen to me children
Please, please listen to me children
Said please, please listen to me
 children
You are the ones who will rule
 the world

Listen to me children
Listen to me children
Please, please listen to me children
Please, please listen to me children
You are the ones who will rule the
 world
You gotta please me
All night

Please, please listen to me children
Said please, please listen to me
 children
Please, yeah, please me
I'm askin' you

Please, please listen to me children
Please, please listen to me children
Please, please listen to me children
Please, my children
Please, children
Please, children

EASY RIDE

And I know
It will be
An easy ride, alright
And I know
It will be
An easy ride, okay

The mask that you wore
My fingers would explore
The costume of control
Excitement soon unfolds

And I know
It will be
An easy ride, yeah
Joy fought vaguely
With your pride
With your pride

Like polished stone
Like polished stone
I see your eyes
Like burning glass
Like burning glass
I hear you smile
Smile, babe

The mask that you wore
My fingers would explore
The costume of control
Excitement soon unfolds

Easy, baby

Coda queen
Now be my bride
Rage in darkness by my side
Seize the summer in your pride
Take the winter in your stride
Let's ride
Easy, easy . . .
All right

WILD CHILD

Wild child
Full of grace
Savior of the human race
Your cool face

Natural child
Terrible child
Not your mother's
Or your father's child
You're our child
Screamin' wild

(An ancient lunatic reigns
in the trees of the night)

With hunger at her heels
Freedom in her eyes
She dances on her knees
Pirate prince at her side
Staring
Into
The hollow idol's eyes

Wild child
Full of grace
Savior of the human race
Your cool face
Your cool face
Your cool face

(Do you remember when we were
in Africa?)

Wild Child

Wild child
Full of grace
Savior of
The human race
your cool face
~~Natural child~~
Terrible child
Not your mother
or your father's
child
You're our child
~~Screaming~~ wild
~~racing thru trees of the night~~
~~Running~~
(spoken: an ancient lunatic reigns in the trees of
~~the night~~
the night)

With hunger at her heels
And freedom in her eyes
She dances on her knees
A pirate prince at her side
~~~~ staring into
The hollow idol's
Eyes.

spoken:
(Remember when
we were in Africa?)

THE SOFT PARADE

When I was back there in seminary
    school
There was a person there
Who put forth the proposition
That you can petition the Lord with
    prayer
Petition the Lord with prayer
Petition the Lord with prayer

You cannot petition the Lord with
    prayer!

Can you give me sanctuary
I must find a place to hide
A place for me to hide

Can you find me soft asylum
I can't make it any more
The man is at the door

Peppermint miniskirts
Chocolate candy
Champion sax
And a girl named Sandy

There's only four ways to get
    unraveled
One is to sleep and the other is
    travel

One is a bandit up in the hills
One is to love your neighbor till
His wife gets home

Catacombs, nursery bones
Winter women growing stones
(Carrying babies to the river)

Streets and shoes, avenues
Leather riders selling news

The monk bought lunch
He bought a little, yes he did
This is the best part of the trip
This is the trip, the best part,
I really like

Successful hills are here to stay
Everything must be this way
Gentle street where people play
Welcome to the soft parade

All our lives we sweat and save
Building for a shallow grave
Must be something else we say
Somehow to defend this place
Everything must be this way
Everything must be this way

The soft parade has now begun
Listen to the engines hum
People out to have some fun
Cobra on my left
Leopard on my right

Deer woman in a silk dress
Girls with beads around their necks
Kiss the hunter of the green vest
Who has wrestled before
With lions in the night

Out of sight

The lights are getting brighter
The radio is moaning
Calling to the dogs
There are still a few animals
Left out in the yard
But it's getting harder
To describe
Sailors
To the underfed

Tropic corridor
Tropic treasure
What got us this far
To this mild equator

We need someone or something
    new
Something else to get us through

Calling on the dogs
Calling on the dogs
Calling on the dogs
Calling in the dogs
Calling all the dogs
Calling on the gods

Meet me at the crossroads
Meet me at the edge of town
Outskirts of the city
Just you and I
And the evening sky
You'd better come alone
You'd better bring your gun
We're gonna have some fun

When all else fails
We can whip the horses' eyes
And make them sleep
And cry. . . .

WHO SCARED YOU

Who scared you?
Why were you born, my babe
Into time's arms with all of
    your charms, my love
Why were you born, just to play
    with me
To freak out or to be beautiful,
    my dear

Load your head, blow it up,
    feeling good, baby
Load your head, blow it up,
    feeling good, baby

Well, my room is so cold
You know you don't have to go,
    my babe
And if you warm it up right
I'm gonna love you tonight,
    my love
Well, I'm glad that we came
I hope you're feeling the same
Who scared you?
And why were you born?
Please stay

I see a rider
Coming down the road
Got a burden
Carrying a heavy load
One sack of silver
And one bag of gold[33]

505

ROADHOUSE BLUES

Keep your eyes on the road
Your hands upon the wheel
Keep your eyes on the road
Your hands upon the wheel
We're goin' to the roadhouse
Gonna have a real good time

Yeah, in back of the roadhouse
They got some bungalows
Yeah, in back of the roadhouse
They got some bungalows
And that's for the people
Who like to go down slow

Let it roll, baby, roll
Let it roll, baby, roll
Let it roll, baby, roll
Let it roll
All night long

Ashen Lady
Ashen Lady
Give up your vows
Give up your vows

Save our city
Save our city
Right now

Well, I woke up this morning
I got myself a beer

Yeah, I woke up this morning
And I got myself a beer
The future's uncertain
And the end is always near

Let it roll, baby, roll
Let it roll, baby, roll
Let it roll, baby, roll
Let it roll
All night long

At first flash of Eden
We raced down to the sea
Standing there on freedom's shore

Waiting for the sun
Waiting for the sun
Waiting for the sun

Can't you feel it, now that spring
    has come
That it's time to live in the
    scattered sun

Waiting for the sun
Waiting for the sun
Waiting for the sun
Waiting for the sun
Waiting . . .

Waiting for you to come along
Waiting for you to hear my song
Waiting for you to come along
Waiting for you to tell me what
went wrong

This is the strangest life I've ever
    known

Can't you feel it, now that spring
    has come
That it's time to live in the
    scattered sun

Waiting for the sun
Waiting for the sun
Waiting for the sun

I really want you, really do
Really need you, baby
God knows I do
Cause I'm not real enough
    without you
Oh, what can I do?

You make me real
You make me feel
Like lovers feel
You make me throw away
Mistake and misery
Make me free, love, make me free

I really want you, really do
Really need you, baby
Really do
I'm not real enough without you
Oh, what can I do?

You make me real
Only you, baby
Have that appeal
So let me slide into
Your tender sunken sea
Make me free, love, make me free

Roll now, baby, roll
You gotta roll now, baby, roll
Roll now, honey, roll
You gotta roll now, baby, roll

You make me real
You make me feel
Like lovers feel
You make me throw away
Mistake and misery
Make me free, love
Make me free
Make me free
You make me free

PEACE FROG

There's blood in the streets, it's up
    to my ankles
Blood in the streets, it's up to
    my knee
Blood in the streets of the town
    of Chicago
Blood on the rise
It's following me

She came. . .
Just about the break of day
She came, then she drove away
Sunlight in her hair

Blood on the streets, runs a river
    of sadness
Blood in the streets, it's up to
    my thigh
The river runs red down the legs
    of the city
The women are crying, red rivers
    of weeping

She came in town
And then she drove away
Sunlight in her hair

Indians scattered
On dawn's highway bleeding
Ghosts crowd
The young child's fragile eggshell
    mind

Blood in the streets in the town of
    New Haven
Blood stains the roofs and the palm
    trees of Venice
Blood in my love in the terrible
    summer
Bloody red sun of fantastic L.A.

Blood screams her brain as they
    chop off her fingers
Blood will be born in the birth of
    a nation
Blood is the rose of mysterious
    union

There's blood in the streets, it's up
    to my ankles
Blood in the streets, it's up to
    my knee
Blood in the streets of the town
    of Chicago
Blood on the rise
It's following me

BLUE SUNDAY

I found my own true love
Was on a blue Sunday
She looked at me and told me
I was the only one in the world
Now I have found my girl

My girl awaits for me in tender time
My girl is mine
She is the world
She is my girl

510

raindrops scattered on dawn's

hiway bleeding. Ghosts
crowd the young child's
fragile eggshell mind
We leag the wall, dog & eye,
to hang clothing on bench
collar chain. Mate follows
leap to suffer hollow
string throat madness
cry! In this hollow we
were born

The human race was dying out
No one left to scream and shout
People walking on the moon
Smog will get you pretty soon

Everyone was hangin' out
Hangin' up and hangin' down
Hangin' in and holdin' fast
Hope our little world will last

Along came Mister Goodtrips
Looking for a new ship
Come on, people, better climb
   on board
Come on, baby, now we're going
   home

Ship of fools
Ship of fools

The human race was dying out
No one left to scream and shout
People walking on the moon
Smog gonna get you pretty soon

Ship of fools
Ship of fools
Ship of fools
Ship of fools
Ship of fools
Ship of fools
Ship of fools

Yeah, climb on board
Ship's gonna leave ya far behind
Climb on board
Ship of fools
Ship of fools

Grandma loved a sailor
Who sailed the frozen sea
Grandpa was that whaler
And he took me on his knee
He said "Son, I'm goin' crazy
From livin' on the land
Got to find my shipmates
And walk on foreign sands"

Now this old man was graceful,
With silver in his smile
He smoked a briar pipe and
He walked four country miles
Singing songs of shady sisters
And old-time liberty
Songs of love and songs of death
And songs to set men free

I've got three ships and sixty men
A course for ports unread
I'll stand at mast, let north
   winds blow
Till half of us are dead

Land ho!

Well, if I get my hands on a
   dollar bill
Gonna buy a bottle and drink
   my fill
If I get my hands on a number five
Gonna skin that little girl alive
If I get my hands on a number two
Come back home and marry you
Marry you
Marry you
All right

Yeah, land ho!
Yeah, land ho!
Well, if I get back home
And I feel all right
You know I'm gonna love
   you tonight
Love tonight
Love tonight
Yeah, land ho!

THE SPY

I'm a spy in the house of love
I know the dreams that you're
   dreamin' of
I know the word that you long
   to hear
I know your deepest secret fear

I'm a spy in the house of love
I know the dreams that you're
   dreamin' of
I know the words that you long
   to hear
I know your deepest secret fear

I know everything
Everything you do
Everywhere you go
Everyone you know

I'm a spy in the house of love
I know the dreams that you're
   dreamin' of
I know the word that you long
   to hear
I know your deepest secret fear
I know your deepest secret fear
I know your deepest secret fear

I'm a spy
I can see you
What you do
And I know

QUEEN OF THE HIGHWAY

She was a princess
Queen of the highway
Sign on the road said
"Take us to Madre"
No one could save her
Save the blind tiger
He was a monster
Black dressed in leather
She was a princess
Queen of the highway

Now they are wedded
She is a good girl
Naked as children
Out in the meadow
Naked as children
Wild as can be
Soon to have offspring
Start it all over
Start it all over

American boy
American girl
Most beautiful people in the world
Son of a frontier Indian swirl
Dancing thru the midnight
   whirlpool
Formless
Hope it can continue a little
   while longer

I love you the best
Better than all the rest
I love you the best
Better than all the rest
That I meet in the summer
Indian summer
That I meet in the summer
Indian summer
I love you the best
Better than all the rest

Miss Maggie M'Gill
She lived on a hill
Her daddy got drunk and left her
    no will
So she went down
Down to Tangie Town
People down there really like to
    get it on

Now if you're sad and you're
    feelin' blue
Go out and buy a brand new pair
    of shoes
And you go down
Down to Tangie Town
The people down there really like
    to get it on
Get it on

Illegitimate son of a rock & roll star
Illegitimate son of a rock & roll star
Mom met Dad in the back of a
        rock & roll car
Yeah

Well, I'm an old blues man
And I think that you understand
I've been singing the blues
Ever since the world began
Yeah

Maggie
Maggie
Maggie M'Gill
Roll on
Roll on
Maggie M'Gill

514

LOVE HIDES

Love hides
In the strangest places
Love hides
In familiar faces

Love comes
When you least expect it
Love hides
In narrow corners
Love comes
For those who seek it
Love hides
Inside the rainbow
Love hides
In molecular structures
Love is the answer

BUILD ME A WOMAN

Give me a witness darlin'
I need a witness, babe
All right
I got the 'poon tang blues, yeah
I got the 'poon tang blues, yeah
Top of my head down
To the bottom of my cowboy shoes

Build me a woman
Make her ten feet tall
You gotta build me a woman
Make her ten feet tall
Don't make her ugly
Don't make her small

You gotta build me a woman
Make her ten feet tall
Build me a woman
Make her ten feet tall
Don't make her ugly
Don't make her small
Build me someone I can ball
All night long

515

UNIVERSAL MIND

I was doing time
In the universal mind
I was feeling fine
I was turning keys
I was setting people free
I was doing all right

Then you came along
With a suitcase and a song
Turned my head around

Now I'm so alone
Just looking for a home
In every face I see

I'm the Freedom Man
I'm the Freedom Man
I'm the Freedom Man
That's how lucky I am

DEAD CATS, DEAD RATS

Dead cats, dead rats
Did ya see what they were at,
   all right
Dead cat in a top hat
Sucking on a young man's blood
Wishing he could come, yeah
Sucking on the soldier's brain
Wishing it would be the same

Dead cat, dead rat
Did ya see what they were at?
Fat cat in a top hat
Thinks he's an aristocrat
Thinks he can kill and slaughter
Thinks he can shoot my daughter

Dead cats, dead rats
Think you're an aristocrat
Crap, that's crap!

THE CHANGELING

I live uptown
I live downtown
I live all around

I had money, I had none
I had money, I had none
But I never been so broke
That I couldn't leave town

I'm a changeling, see me change
I'm a changeling, see me change

I'm the air you breathe
Food you eat
Friends you greet
In the swarming street

See me change, see me change

I live uptown
I live downtown
I live all around

I had money, yeah, I had none
I had money, yeah, I had none
But I never been so broke
That I couldn't leave town

I'm the air you breathe
Food you eat
Friends you greet
In the swarming street

See me change, see me change

I'm leaving town
On the midnight train
Gonna see me change, change,
    change
Change, change, change
Change, change, change

BEEN DOWN SO LONG

Well, I been down so goddamn long
That it looks like up to me
Well, I been down so very damn
  long
That it looks like up to me
Now, why don't one of you people
C'mon and set me free?

I said, warden, warden, warden
Won't you break your lock & key
I said, warden, warden, warden
Won't you break your lock & key
Hey, come along here, mister
C'mon and let the poor boy be

Baby, baby, baby
Won't you get down on your knees
Baby, baby, baby
Won't you get down on your knees
C'mon little darlin'
C'mon and give your love to me
Oh, yeah

Well, I been down so goddamn long
That it looks like up to me
Well, I been down so very damn
  long
That it looks like up to me
Now why don't one of you people
C'mon, c'mon, c'mon
And set me free!

CARS HISS BY MY WINDOW

The cars hiss by my window
Like the waves down on the beach
The cars hiss by my window
Like the waves down on the beach
I got this girl beside me
But she's out of reach

Headlights thru my window
Shining on the wall
Headlights thru my window
Shining on the wall
Can't hear my baby
Tho' I call and call

Window started tremblin'
With those sonic booms
Window started to tremble
With those sonic booms, boom
A cold girl'll kill you
In a darkened room

Cars hiss by my window
  like The
      waves down on the beach (2)
I've got this girl beside me
  but she's out of reach

Headlights thru my window
  Shining on the wall (2)
I can't hear my baby tho I
  call & call
      (~~vocal call~~)

Window starts to Tremble
  w/a sonic boom (2)
A cold girl will kill you in a
  darkened room

Dogs are roaming in the
      cruel morning yard (2)
To lose your love & keep
  That's more than hard

Well she feels like dying
But she's only 21 (2)
she's not alone man
  she's not the only one.

L.A. WOMAN

Well, I just got into town about
    an hour ago
Took a look around, see which way
    the wind blow
Where the little girls in their
    Hollywood bungalows
Are you a lucky little lady in the
    City of Light?
Or just another lost angel

City of night, City of night
City of night, City of night

L.A. woman, L.A. woman
L.A. woman, Sunday afternoon
L.A. woman, Sunday afternoon

L.A. woman, Sunday afternoon
Drive thru your suburbs
Into your blues
Into your blues
Into your blue, blue, blues
Into your blues

I see your hair is burning
Hills are filled with fire
If they say I never loved you
You know they are a liar

Drivin' down your freeways
Midnight alleys roam
Cops in cars, the topless bars
Never saw a woman so alone
So alone, so alone, so alone

Motel Money Murder Madness
Let's change the mood
From glad to sadness

Mr. Mojo risin'
Mr. Mojo risin'
Mr. Mojo risin'
Mr. Mojo risin'
Got to keep on risin'
Mr. Mojo risin'
Mr. Mojo risin'
Mr. Mojo risin'
Got my Mojo risin'
Mr. Mojo risin'
Got to keep on risin'
Goin' ridin', 'ridin'
Goin' ridin', 'ridin'
Got to ridin', ridin'
Ridin', ridin'

Well, I just got into town about
    an hour ago
Took a look around, see which way
    the wind blow
Where the little girls in their
    Hollywood bungalows
Are you a lucky little lady in the
    City of Light?
Or just another lost angel

City of night
City of night
City of night
City of night

L.A. woman, L.A. woman
L.A. woman
You're my woman

A little L.A. woman, L.A. woman
Hey, hey, come on
L.A. woman, come on

J.M. / Doors

L.A. Woman

Well, I just got into town about
an hour ago

Took a look around, see which
way the wind blow

Where the little girls in their
Hollywood bungalows

Are you a lucky little lady in
the City of Light?

Or just another lost angel
City of Night (4)

L.A. Woman (4) (2)

L.A. Woman Sunday afternoon (3)

Drive thru your suburbs

Into your blues (4) (2)

Into your blue-blue Blues

Into your blues

L'AMERICA

I took a trip down to L'America
To trade some beads for a pint
   of gold
I took a trip down to L'America
To trade some beads for a pint
   of gold

L'America, L'America, L'America
L'America, L'America, L'America

C'mon people, don't you look
   so down
You know the rainman's comin'
   to town
He'll change your weather
He'll change your luck
Then he'll teach you
How to find yourself
L'America

Friendly strangers came to town
All the people put them down
But the women loved their ways
Come again some other day
Like the gentle rain
Like the gentle rain that falls

I took a trip down to L'America
To trade some beads for a pint
   of gold
I took a trip down to L'America
To trade some beads for a pint
   of gold

L'America, L'America, L'America
L'America, L'America, L'America

HYACINTH HOUSE

What are they doing in the
   Hyacinth house
What are they doing in the
   Hyacinth house
To please the lions this day?

I need a brand-new friend who
   doesn't bother me
I need a brand-new friend who
   doesn't trouble me
I need someone, who doesn't
   need me

I see the bathroom is clear
I think that somebody's near
I'm sure that someone is
   following me
Oh, yeah

Why did you throw the
   Jack-of-Hearts away?
Why did you throw the
   Jack-of-Hearts away?
It was the only card in the deck
That I had left to play

And I'll say it again
I need a brand-new friend
And I'll say it again
I need a brand-new friend
And I'll say it again
I need a brand-new friend
The end

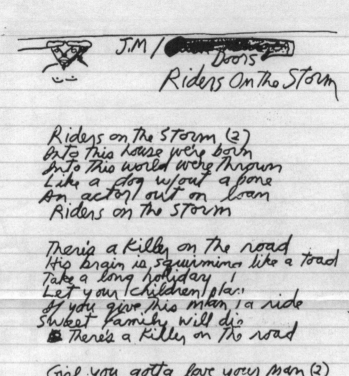

J.M / Doors
Riders On The Storm

Riders on The Storm (2)
Into this house we're born
Into this world we're thrown
Like a dog w/out a bone
An actor out on loan
Riders on The Storm

There's a Killer on The road
His brain is squirming like a toad
Take a long holiday
Let your children play
If you give this man a ride
Sweet family will die
There's a Killer on The road

Girl you gotta love your man (2)
Take him by The hand
Make him understand
The world on you depends
Our life will never end
Girl you gotta love your man

(Repeat 1).

Riders on the Storm (4)

THE WASP
(TEXAS RADIO AND THE BIG BEAT)

I want to tell you about Texas Radio
    and the Big Beat
Comes out of the Virginia swamps
Cool and slow, with plenty of
    precision,
And a back beat narrow and hard
    to master
Some call it heavenly in its
    brilliance.
Others, mean and rueful of the
    Western dream

I love the friends I have gathered
    together
On this thin raft
We have constructed pyramids
In honor of our escaping
This is the land where the
    Pharaoh died

The Negroes in the forest brightly
    feathered
And they are saying:
"Forget the night!
Live with us in forests of azure
Out here on the perimeter, there are
    no stars
Out here we is stoned—
    immaculate."

Listen to this, I'll tell you about
    the heartache,
I'll tell you about heartache and
    the loss of God
I'll tell you about the hopeless night
The meager food for souls forgot
Tell you about the maiden with
    wrought iron soul
I'll tell you this
No eternal reward can forgive
    us now
For wasting the dawn.

I'll tell you about Texas Radio
    and the Big Beat
Soft-driven, slow and mad like
    some new language
Now listen to this, I'll tell you
    about Texas
I'll tell you about Texas Radio
I'll tell you about the hopeless night
The wanderin' the Western dream
Tell you about the maiden with
    wrought iron soul

RIDERS ON THE STORM

Riders on the storm, riders on
    the storm
Into this house we're born
Into this world we're thrown
Like a dog without a bone
An actor out on loan
Riders on the storm

There's a killer on the road
His brain is squirming like a toad
Take a long holiday
Let your children play
If you give this man a ride
Sweet family will die
Killer on the road

Girl, you gotta love your man
Girl, you gotta love your man
Take him by the hand
Make him understand
The world on you depends
Our life will never end
Gotta love your man

Riders on the storm, riders on
    the storm
Into this house we're born
Into this world we're thrown
Like a dog without a bone
An actor out on loan
Riders on the storm

I want to tell you
about
Texas Radio & The Big Beat

it comes out of the Virginia swamps
cool & slow
w/ plenty of precision
& a back beat narrow
& hard to master

some call it heavenly —
in its brilliance
others mean & rueful
of the Western dream

— I love the friends I have
gathered together
on this thin raft
we have constructed pyramids
in honor of our escaping
This is the land where
the pharoah died —

Children
The river contains specimens
The voices of singing women

From *Backstage and Dangerous: The Private Rehearsal* January 2002

I will never be untrue
Do anything you would want me to
Never stay out drinking
No later than two, two-thirty

I will never treat you mean
And I won't cause no kind of scene
Tell you all the people
All the places I have been

I will always treat you kind
Try to give you peace of mind
If only you tell me that you love me
One more time

Now darling, please don't be sad
Don't run off like that when you
   get mad
'Cause if you do, you gonna lose
The best friend that you ever had
That's no lie

530

I will never be untrue
Do everything you want me to do
Bring all my loving, all my money
Bring it all home to you

SOMEDAY SOON

Someday soon, someday soon
Familiar freaks will fill your
    living room
Rugs lash out with their
    lizard tongues
You're not getting young
You're not getting young

And I hate to remind you
But you're going to die
And you're going to be needing
All of your eyes

You'll be all alone
When the animals cry
All by yourself
In the infancy's lie

Someday soon, someday soon
Television bleeding like a
    harvest moon
Flush the scissors down the hole
You're getting old
You're getting old

And I hate to remind you
But you're going to die
And you're going to be needing
All of your lies

You'll be all alone
When the animals cry
All by yourself
In the infancy's lie

Someday soon, someday soon
Someday soon, someday soon

I like to write. I'm even publishing a book of my poems pretty soon, stuff I had that I realized wasn't for music. But songs are special; I find that music liberates my imagination. When I sing my songs in public, that's a dramatic act, but not just acting as in theater, but as a social act, real action.[34]

MAGIC OF YOUR MIND

Magic of your mind
Butterfly Way
Music of your dragstrip
charms
Insulated scene
Tragic viewpt.
News show roundup
Succeed where others fail

Lonesome Romance
Hobo in a Trance
Get down on the line

Favorable sign
Oval village mine
insulated garbage pail
broken-down rhyme

WHO SCARED YOU

Who scared you
Why were you born   533
Into time's arms
w/all your charms
Why were you born
to play w/me
to freak out or be beautiful

I'm glad you came
I'm glad you've come
I'm glad I came
I'm glad I've come
I'm glad we came
I'm glad we've come

But who scared you
Why were you born
Into time's arms
w/all your charms

THE ALLIGATOR MAN

Well now the alligator Man
has come to call
He's got a snakeskin jacket
an eye, & a claw
He's got a sack hung
round his horse's neck
& he's got a pistol
& he's got a red dog
that comes when he whistles
He's the alligator Man
& he's come to call (2)
Selling skins & furs
& powder & balls

I'LL NEVER GIVE

I'll never give
your secret
away

I've been waiting
so long
To hold you
in my arms

And I'll never
give your secret
away

I will never
be unkind
I'll give you
Peace of mind
Thru the evening
& part of the day

I KNOW YOU'VE BEEN

I know you've been
sad & blue
I know just what you've been
going thru
I can
see that faraway look
in your eyes
I can sit here &
I surmise

You've been witnessed
You've seen your birth
You've been treasured
& I can guess
You're on your way home to me

I can see now
that I was wrong
Kind of blinded
by your eyes
It was evil
Feel inside
The more I'm blinded, the more
    I see
Come back baby, & sing to me (4)

She's returning w/her packages
She's returning w/her magic
She's returning w/her moron face
& simple world

She's coming back (8)

But not until
The 4th of July

SEVEN YEARS OF BLIGHT

Yes, 7 yrs blight & stuff like that
I see ya
dogs bark & cymbals crash
I need ya
Lightening flash the frogs forget
I'll leave ya
April's gone - Tomorrows frown
I'll see ya
This chance forget I'll see you yet
G'bless you
And no one fret, decrease my debt
in Limbo
Our souls amaze
our souls surprise
I'll leave you
No well to moan
No more to

BLACK CAT BONE

Black Cat Bone (7)

All alone -----------

Largest partner in the
Universe

Got my Mojo working
Got my baby's mother's blood
I got the good Lord
in my pocket, yes

No one's going to trouble me
No one's going to bother me
No more

Ghosts in the hall
Timberline & waterfall
Medicine will not help
at all

I Know you've been / Sad & blue
I Know just what you've been / going thru
I can/see that faraway look / in your eyes
I can sit here & / & surmise

You've been witnessed
you've ~~been~~ seen your birth
you've been treasured
   & I can guess
you're on your way home to me

I can see now / that I was wrong
Kind of blinded / by your eyes
It was evil
Feel inside
The more I'm blinded, the more I see
Come back baby, & sing to me (4) (1)

She's returning w/ her packages
She's returning w/her magic
She returning w/ her moron face
& simple world

She's coming back (8)

But not until
The 4th of July

ARNOLD DERWIN, M.D.
9400 BRIGHTON WAY
BEVERLY HILLS, CALIFORNIA

James Morrison
2522 Verbena Drive
Los Angeles, California

BEVERLY HILLS
28 JUN
1969

THE HOOK

She lives down
on by gone
Street

Smokes nylon
cigarets
Sweet love
The hook

Can't tell you all
the love she
took
The hook

Ancient molecules
Rearview Turnpikes
The hook

Can't tell you all
the love she
took
The hook (2)

Hard as a willow
Wolfin weepin
Tree

Took me home
Made a friend
of me
The hook

Surprise all the
love she took
The hook

She's fine
The hook

1 dollar on the
table
a dollar on the
line
Shake your ass
Mr. President
She's mine

I mean
The hook

10 pachookos
in the back of
a car
She's raped again
like a star
I mean the hook

Lone tall
Soul sister

Last call
gentlemen
What you
want to do

Love's
in vain

WENT INTO A BARROOM

Went into a barroom
down in Tacoland
South of Texas border
Cross the Rio Grande

The place it was called Boy's Town
Known for miles around
10 cent beer & give a cheer
young girls were to be found

The juke box took my quarter
K-9 on the dial
Surveyed the room, & pretty soon
I spied a Southern smile

Now its hightime we boogied
& its high old time we railed
Against the stupid system
& the fools who had us jailed

GOT A REAL FINE WOMAN

I got a real fine
woman
She's got Sunday
in the oven
Got a crystal-hearted
mind
& she's cryin all the
time

Mentholated breath
Not afraid of death

W/her patchwork face
Like a pink & black
puppy
Good-time girl,
Makes me feel quite
lucky

Shoot the man down (3)

WITCH SONG

Now how could I name
the spell she claimed
A witch come womb come wivey
If witch was her name
Then how could she claim
To know me like a Navey

I was a boy who came to a Man
The man said witch com wivey
All of my mates were chortling
    snakes
In the face of witch com wivey

I will not a go
like the other's will go
I watch a witch com wivey
I got on my horse as a matter
of course, & rode to meet my Lady

I lay'd w/her & dug her fur
as fits a proper lady
But as everyman knows
w/feet in his toes
He does not make a baby

She settled it once
She settled it twice
& sent me on my way-o
This ridiculous verse
May mean my hearse
if her baby's borne a boyo

O come w/me
To see my Love
In harbor on the bay-o
The bay of Life or Bay of death
Me not cares what you call-o
Shoot the man down (3)

The Hook ①

She lives down
 on bygone
        street
Smokes nylon
    cigareets
Sweet love
  The hook
Can't tell you all
  The love she
       Took
   The hook
Ancient molecules
Rearview Turnpikes
  The hook
Can't tell you all
   The love she
        took
  The hook (2)

Hard as a willow
Wolfin weepin
Thee
Took me home
Made a friend
of me
The hook
Surprin all the
love she took
The hook

She's fine
The hook
1 dollar on the
Table
9 dollar on the
line
Shake your ass
Mr President
She's mine
& mean
The hook

10 pachookos
in the back of
a car
She's raped again
like a star
& mean The hook

Lone tall
soul sister

Last call
gentlemen

Up of man
not famly
Loved
in vain

& don't want her
you can have her
She's to much
harder

N'S SONG

Now once there was
fair Irish lad
Young Nicolas was his name
He took his name from
former fame
& made his talents flame

Now he had grit & he had wit
& on him it did show
He took no joke from any a bloke
but toked it just the same

And if any a gal could catch his eye
he'd win her in a troth
He was the son of someone dead
Fair Nicolas was his name

Now ye've spied upon poor Willie
Ye've looked upon yon Dan
But nary a spoke you've give
    or took
Till Nicolas came along
(refrain)

O different strokes
for different folks
But all (the) young
(quite) seem able

Who'll fight fools w/fire
& Who'll fight fools w/flame
Not I, Not I, says anyman
But I'll fight 'im jest the same

(& you know it too brother
you know what I mean)
HE STOLE FROM ME

WHERE ARE YOU?

Where are you
Where are you

I need you
I seek you
Everywhere

I was standing on The Highway
(Cold morning - warm evening
Hot, City, Noon)
I was standing on the Highway
(repeat)

All that light, all that
bright hot light
had baked my shadow gray

Then you drove by
(In your) wine blue racer
You picked me up
You fed me your hair
Your eyes, your mouth

You turned around
& headed South (3)

T.J.!
(Party lights)
L A
The City of Night
Ensenada
Night of the Moon
The Sea & The Stars
Cooked in a spoon (3)

Where are you
I look everywhere
I seek your hair
on concrete stairs

I seek your eyes
in melting skies
I seek your mouth
in the Journey South (3)

Are you in Sun City
City of Lights
Are you a Lost Angel
in the City of Night

Where are you
Why did you leave
You picked me up
Made a man of me
& Now you're gone
Now you're not here (2)

I miss your hair
I miss your mouth
I miss your eyes
I miss your eyes smiling
in the Melting Sky

You're gone
Disappeared
Somewhere in that desert
Somewhere in that Motel Night

I'm waiting for her laugh
When she strips off the mask
Nose Mouth eyes
Nose Mouth eyes

What surprise
in the order of their telling
The brain's telling
me
To go somewhere
To do something
(even the hand rebels
& seeks rivers
of schools & jails)

What is it telling me
What is she saying?

I'm looking for the girl
I saw in my dream
(on a highway
picked me up)
I'm waiting for her laugh
The hard soft stroke
of her ass
Kneeling, her thighs,
& her back
Tense a thin sliver
silk

Where will I find you?
Where can I call?
Over the window,
Under the Hall?
Beside the beach
Against the Town?
My mind skips a week
at your slightest frown

Hey, little girl
you're lookin fine
Like to make the
little girl mine

Won't you come to call
won't you come to call
won't you come, hon
    & bring it all
I'm so upset & so alone
won't you come &
    bring it all home

HEY LITTLE GIRL

Hey, little girl
You're lookin fine
Like to make the
Little girl mine

Won't you come to call
Won't you come to call
Won't you come hon
& bring it all

I'm so upset & so alone
Won't you come &
bring it all home

Give me a sign (3)
Give me a look
Send me a book
drop me a line
Cause I'm so uptight

GENTLEMEN MADMEN ALL

Gentlemen Madmen all (2)
Hear me when I call

Gather together at the sunrise (2)
For the wedding of our soul(s)

I need your promised lightening
I need your borrowed gold
I need the silence of the sunrise
& a glimpse of pasts untold

Come on (8)

I got my foot in the door
Stick my shirt on the wall
Move down the hallway

Move over

THE DESERT

I

Landscape of the heart
The desert of your mind
As long as we're apart
We'll keep the earth in flames

II

But when the sun & I are wed
Lay'd down in the Western night
[Then the sky will have its voice
And the earth its evening rain]

(change)
And the rain came down!

repeat 1

SWEET TEARS

Sweet tears (2)
To bind us
& water us well

Bottle of
Sweet tears
calling to me
Sweet tears
down the way, & all
thru the years

The rock
The big rock
writing on the surface
w/these
Sweet tears (2)

545

THE WALKING BLUES

I've got the walking blues
Low-down mean ol' walkin' blues
I got them in the bottom of
my walkin' shoes

You know I'm just down here
on a visit
And I'm gonna leave if you
don't soon quit it
all this messin' around
burnin' the town
Fightin & Killin & lootin & shootin'
I'm leavin' town

DEEP FREEZE BLUES

Deep freeze blues
Chocolate shoes
Whole lot of money &
Nothing to lose
Whole lot of lovin'
& trouble & news
I'm lying in the ocean
w/the deep freeze blues

I LIKE THE WAY

I like the way you do your hair
I love the color of your underwear
I love your milky silky snow
white breast
Your car your jar of coke
& your Sunday best
Keep your soul locked in
the closet hon
I brought my sub-machine
gun rifle knife & saw
Don't mess w/me cause
I'm the LAW

ALL AROUND THE MORNIN'

All round the mornin'
all round the evenin'
all round country side

People get children
Children get wisdom
Children goin learn to ride
All right
now

Wisdom is narrow
wisdom is nothin'
nothin but an evil tooth ride
But sickness is sorrow (2)
This gonna be our last time

Get home for rooster
get back for dinner
Take your last little bike ride
all rite (4)

THE WEDDING DRESS

Coda Queen
Be my Bride
Rage in darkness
By my side
Seize the summer in your pride
Take the winter in your stride

Meet me
At the Crossroads
Meet me
at the edge of town
Just you & I
& the evening sky
You better come alone

THE IDIOT ROARS

The idiot roars, in laughter
out my door (2)
And strange things happened
out those doors
About which I'll tell you
more & more

Like guerrilla warfare
on your mind
You plow into it from behind

It's filled w/Brothers
It's filled w/Lovers
It's filled w/Fathers
And smiling Sisters
It's filled w/layer after layer
of frightening Mothers

(Scream)

burrow back thru that
comic past
burrow back thru that
cartoon past
burrow back thru that
gray T.V. past
burrow back into that
radio dark night
burrow back beyond all
that
burrow back, burrow back

Take a journey w/me
to the
WEST!

(girls scream;
Singer laughs, sighs,
out of breath
band glides on)

Every trip is a trip
that I know
Every trip is a trip
we are told
But a trip is only a trip
A trip is never a journey

And journeys are better
than trips
But journeys mean
Numbers & Numbers
And take quite a lot of time

But don't leave you stranded
on some foreign shore
looking around, asking for more

NOW BACK AT THE BEACH

Now back at the beach
At the top of the sun
We fall in the sand
& greet everyone

Where have we been
They all want to know
And so we tell them:

It isn't high or low
it isn't near or far
it's not hard to get there
But you can't go by car

You'll know it when you see it
I'll show you the Way
It's not hard to do it
Listen to me play

SOLO

(childishly works up scales
false climax
band leaps to new key
break into higher cleaner loftier air
-or merely stranger)

Now you're there
up in the air
Your body's light
Your brain is clear
You're on a flight
To the end of the night

Take the Hiway to the
End of the Night
End of the night (2)

Take a Journey to the
Bright Midnight
End of the Night (2)

Hold on tight
(while we)
fall thru the Night (2)

Hold on tight
Hold on tight
Hold on tight
Hold on tight

It's time to ignite
The Carnival lights
Try to set the night on fire

Learn to explore
Beyond the door
Try to set the night on fire

Try to excite
A cry in the night
Try to set the night on fire (3)

SHE'S A BALL-BREAKER

She's a Ball-breaker
hard-hearted Undertaker
Knows exactly what she wants
She knows where we came
from

She knows -
(yes knows) (3)
She knows where we came
from
She's a crook'd hearted
#g
Thing for sure & looks
real fine
Ambulator - perculator
You know she feels fine
& I know
(yes, how I know) (3)
I know she feels love

HOUSES

O, in the house where I was born
it was on a shady morn
& the light shone from a candle
that came streaming off the mantle
& caught me crying like a baby
just out from mother's arms
O, it was certain astral-jection
Sure no place for little boys

So I put on my red sweater
& went running to the window
Looking out there was a daughter
lovely of our next door neighbor

Got me righteous, got me dizzy
She got me full of loco weed
& so I grabbed her behind the barn
& I commenced to fill her needs

STAY STAY STAY

Stay Stay Stay
My cheery young girl
Stay for the nights a grievin'
I'm still a million miles from home
a million miles from Eden

From Eden's glen I sore did ride
& got 5 score of children
Has anyone seen the strap she wore
or felt her full chill screechin;

Hoot owl coos & soothes the morn
a winkled eye did waken
Off we gang to another spire
off to the Midland racin'

QUEEN OF THE MAGAZINES

I wish I was a girl of 16
I'd be the Queen of the Magazines
I'd be a Movie Star
I'd drive a brand new car
I'd see the World as a great big
    dream
And all night long you could hear
me scream

TO BE ALONE

To be alone
& watch the dawn
It could create
a silly song
About a girl
I used to know

She was the star
of the lost side show

She wasn't me
She wasn't you
Believe you me
Knew what to do

& say to a man on
the end of his tether
"Hey, fine handsome
Man, there'll be a change
in the weather"

So what am I
Supposed to do
Just sit alone
& chew my shoe
I need a love
No more than she
& yet no less
& no regrets

PALACE IN THE CANYON

There's a palace
in the canyon
where you & I
were born

Now I'm a lonely man
Take me back into
the Garden

Blue Shadows
Of the Canyon
I met you
& now you're gone

& now my dream is gone
Let me back into your Garden

(musical break)

A man searching
for lost Paradise
Can seem a fool
to those who never
sought the other world

Where friends do lie
& drift insanely
In their own
In their own
private gardens

There's a palace
in the canyon
I met you
And now you're gone

And now my love is gone
Let me back into
your Garden

Blue Shadows
In the Canyon
I met you
& now you're gone

& now my dream is gone
Let me back into your Garden

To me a song comes with the music, a sound or rhythm first, then I make up words as fast as I can just to hold on to the feel until actually the music and the lyric come almost simultaneously. With a poem there's not necessarily any music . . . a sense of rhythm and in that sense, a kind of music, but a song is more primitive. Usually it has a rhyme and a basic meter, whereas a poem can go anywhere.[35]

V

EPILOGUE

AS I
LOOK BACK

As I look back
        over my life
        I am struck by post cards
        Ruined snap shots
                faded posters
        Of a time, I can't recall

Before the beach, & birth,
        was the home for travelers
        juvenile pen
        a barracks in limbo
        of souls sans desire

They instill desire, day by day
        & night too

Parachute birth
1st moments as war
1st days of pain

Struggle toward
consciousness

I am a Scot, or so
I'm told. Really
the heir of Mystery
                Christians

The child of a
        Military family . . . .

1st early memories
— attention-getting
baby hide from mother
& elephant walk

back thru time to that child
        again, staring rotten
                thru the fence at the angels
                        next door

early memories
Asthma
Albuquerque lawn chairs & lock'd
     in garage shelves w/girl
Beautiful Mexican girl - her mother
May dance - lost shoe
"Bad boy" - No, he's a good boy
Think of Nothing - get what you want
The Mail Box

I initiated dirt-clod
fights in the canyon
& got bombed in the
stomach by rocks

Parachutes from silk
handkerchief

Kites

Snake in the Glen

"But they were picking
    on the little kids"

I told stories & led
Treasure hunts for children

I led bicycle packs
chasing girls home from
school & delighted in
spanking them

I rebelled against church
    after phases of
        fervor

V. EPILOGUE: AS I LOOK BACK

I curried favor in school
       & attack'd the teachers

          I was given a
          desk in the corner

          I was a fool
                  &
          The smartest kid
             in class

I created a mock treasure
Tried to get blood
To hide in woods near school
a monitor stopt me

Walks in D.C. in
             Negro streets. The library
             & book stores. Orange
             brick in warm sun.
             The books & poets magic

Then sex gives greater stimulation
Than you've ever known &
all peace & books lose their
charm & you are thrown
back on the eye of vision

chooks - depantsing - fights - Blue Bus etc.

Trying to have a ducktail

asserted myself by wit

I have tried to learn more about
homos but it's not easy to discuss.

This is true about sex in general,
even more than philosophy or religion

Morés change - but not the mystery

History of Rock
     coinciding w/my
          adolescence

Came to LA to
  Film School

I was never really
  much of a doper

Acid popular, taken at least once or twice
by most everyone I knew
  "grinding your wheels"

I can attest to its power. Saw many
astonishing things

Venice Summer

Drug Visions

Roof top songs

558

The early Notebook
Lost Notebooks

Watching Elvis on T.V.
humorous R & R riots

Name came 1st
Doors of Perception

Our lugubrious snaky
sound. Heavy as ice
as glass.

V. EPILOGUE: AS I LOOK BACK

early struggles &
                    humiliations

Thanks to the girls
who fed me.

Making Records

Elvis had sex - wise
mature voice at 19.

Mine still retains the
nasal whine of a
repressed adolescent
        minor squeaks & furies
An interesting singer
at best - a scream
or a sick croon. Nothing
in-between.

It's hard, this going back

Tropicana - naked
        Acid. Christ, it's
you, a female human.   559

Bo Diddley

Them

London Fog

Whisky - the girls cheated Box office

Love

ROAD DAYS

fear of Plane death

And night was what Night
                should be
A girl, a bottle, & blessed sleep

Night of the End

-- does no one understand

wreck studio

A natural leader, a poet,
a Shaman, w/the
soul of a clown.

My desire for family

What am I doing
   in the Bull Ring
            Arena
Every public figure
    running for Leader

Spectators at the Tomb
 -riot watchers

Fear of Eyes
Assassination

Artaud's effort
to escape the collective
                consciousness

I have ploughed
My seed thru the heart
of the nation.
        Injected a germ in the psychic blood vein.

Now I embrace the poetry
of business & become - for
a time - a "Prince of Industry"

Had the disgrace to
be successful.
Back Door Man
Never tipped over into
revolutionary hysteria.

1st to bring normal
academic intelligence
to rock. Classical
                American

I sit looking out
office window movie
The soft parade

Longhairs
bands over the city
  gangs of outlaws

The meeting

Rid of managers & agents

The horror of business

Public self- analysis

The Problem of Money
    guilt
   do I deserve it?

Being drunk is a good disguise.

I drink so I
can talk to assholes.
This includes me.

Miami blew my confidence
   but really I blew it
     on purpose

The Decency Rally
"And away we go."

The Jury - Sniffing the Witnesses
Trying the Devil in Florida

   Fear of Jail
   "No, you'd adjust."

   Relief of trial (bearable)
   & pleasant life here.

V. EPILOGUE: AS I LOOK BACK

each day is a drive thru history

regret for wasted nights
        & wasted years
I pissed it all away
        American Music

After 4 yrs. I'm left w/a
        mind like a fuzzy hammer

Milton's youth
-- will I get a
chance to write my
    Paradise Lost

    To break w/past (wife
    & partners) & define self.

    The joy of performing has
    ended.
    Joy of films is pleasure
    of writing.

End w/fond good-bye
& plans for future
--Not an actor
    writer - filmmaker

Money from home
    good luck
    stay out of trouble

Which of my cellves
        will be remember'd

Good-bye America
    I loved you[36]

Seasons Greetings

Steve, Clara
Jimmy & Anne